ONCE UPON A STARTUP

HOW TO START YOUR ECOMMERCE BUSINESS AND THRIVE

DANIELLE SADY

KMD
BOOKS

Cover design by Dylan Ingram

Typeset in Adobe Garamond Pro 12.5/18pt

NATIONAL LIBRARY OF AUSTRALIA

A catalogue record for this work is available from the National Library of Australia

National Library of Australia Catalogue-in-Publication data:

Once Upon a Startup/Danielle Sady

ISBN: 978-0-6456278-0-0
(Paperback)

The role of 'entrepreneur' is so demanding and challenging that it can't possibly be done. Thats why it's important to think of the role as 'causing the realisation of your vision'. Its actually about your power to have and communicate a compelling vision and to attract the talented individuals you need into a cohesive and rewarding community.

Danielle reached out to me early in her journey, and I have been pleased to be a small part of her business community.

Stefan Preston
Entrepreneur

DEDICATION

I want to dedicate this book to firstly to my parents. Thank you for opening my world up to the possibilities and opportunities you both did. You showed me that I can achieve anything I put my mind to. Your knowledge, spirit and belief in me has allowed me to dream big and strive for my goals. I am forever grateful for everything you have done for me. I can only hope that you will forever see the determination I proudly inherited from you both.

Sal, thank you for your unwavering support and for being the best sounding board I could ask for. This book was an idea I threw around and it was you who believed in me and encouraged me to pursue it, thank you. Love you always, Kralim.

To my beautiful children, Aaliyah, Kanye, Zaharra and Ziya. Thank you for being the most amazing children I could ever ask for and for teaching me that I don't need to be perfect, I just need to be there. I am forever your biggest cheerleaders in life.

To the wonderful mentors I have had the privilege of working with to date, you all know who you are. Regardless of how big or small you feel your input was I am so grateful that you shared your time, knowledge and network with me – it helped me so much. Thank you from the bottom of my heart.

To Karen, my amazing publisher, and all the team at KMD publishing, from the moment we met it felt so right to work with you and trust you with my work. Thank you for believing in me and what my book was about. Thank you for helping me share my knowledge with so many incredible readers around the world.

To Faye, Carolynne and Alison, thank you for your support and for offering me encouragement to keep writing.

Finally, to you, my incredible reader. Thank you from the bottom of my heart for selecting my book. I truly value your time and am so grateful that you have allowed me to share with you what I have learned on my journey and hope that you get so much knowledge from every page. I am beyond thrilled to have this opportunity and hope that you enjoy every moment reading this book just like I did when writing it for you. I cannot wait to hear all about your journeys and wish you every success.

Danielle

xxx

CONTENTS

Dedication v

Introduction 1

Chapter 1: The Groundwork 13

Chapter 2: The Market and How You Will Stand Out 24

Chapter 3: Your Unique Selling Position 32

Chapter 4: Name and Registration Please 39

Chapter 5: Your Brand is Much More than a Logo 49

Chapter 6: Make it Official 61

Chapter 7: Product or Service 73

Chapter 8: The Dollars and Cents 86

Chapter 9: Stock Management 99

Chapter 10: Your website and first impression 109

Chapter 11: Social Media 135

Chapter 12: Influencers, Brand Ambassadors and Collaborations 154

Chapter 13: Mindset 166

Chapter 14: Your Schedule 178

Chapter 15: Policies, Procedures and Templates 187

Chapter 16: Sales Planning & Strategy: What, When and How 204

Chapter 18: Wholesale 216

Chapter 19: Launching 228

Chapter 20: Selling Through Third Parties.............................234
Chapter 21: You (Education and Growth).............................245
Conclusion...254

INTRODUCTION

'That's the real trouble with the world.
Too many people grow up.' – Walt Disney

Most kids, as they grow up, play their imaginary games of school, Barbies or board games, but for me, I would sell people cars and imagine running my own businesses. I had our playroom at home set up like an office at the dealership with a make-believe switchboard using a semi-broken keyboard and an old home phone receiver. I would use outdated invoice books and walk around our home selling people cars from the range. This was fun for me and gave me passion and joy every moment; the image was real to me, and I couldn't wait for my future. I was determined to be a business owner.

I started working for my dad in 2001 when a full-time role opened up in the admin team. Yes, I had to interview for the role with the general manager and was paid the minimum data entry role wage. It was very clear that I was not receiving special treatment whilst being employed, and when I was late, I definitely knew about it. Which was often, I will admit. I lived around the corner but always seemed to be late. I think it was a maturity thing for me, at that point I was overconfident but didn't realise until much later in life that I needed to stop and focus on the opportunity in front of me, to really try and allow my full potential to blossom. Nonetheless, that is definitely part of the journey, and to me, life was pretty much perfect. My childhood dream was coming true – until it wasn't.

I will always remember the day in 2005 I thought my entire world had come crashing down. My dad had decided it was time to sell the business and semiretire. I was gutted. My dream was gone, what was I going to do? I didn't know what or where I would go and work once the sale was finalised. In that moment, I did not know that it was the best thing that could have happened to me and my career. It set me off on a voyage of discovery that would in turn lead me, in 2021, to sitting in my office having founded two startup businesses and writing my first book to share all the education and lessons I have learned. It's so surreal saying those words out loud. I am so freaking excited to be sharing what I have learned in the hope that I can help you and so many aspiring business owners learn from my journey and my mistakes.

I found many courses and online programs that could help in different areas but struggled to find one solid resource to talk about the variety of areas collectively that need to be thought about when setting up a business, in particular an ecommerce store. So many times I felt alone, defeated – and suffered imposter syndrome, that shit is real. Even when you're winning it can rear its ugly head, but when something doesn't work, it can grow to the size of King Kong and try and derail you. Know you are not alone.

It was a spring day in 2012, and I was sitting at my dining table, finishing some work, feeling deflated from a shopping experience I had had that day. I had been out for work at a local department store when I made a quick stop at the lingerie department after my meeting. There was not one pair of underwear that suited or fit me. I questioned what was wrong with me and drove home sad and irritated. The light bulb flicked on. *Hang on,* I remember thinking. *If there is no company making what I need, I will go and make the underwear I need myself; I am sure there are others who are in the same boat.*

I went about asking everyone I knew about their underwear – what they are after; what they would want; how they want to feel. I began learning so much about the underwear industry from those close to me, so I took it one step further and joined some networking groups where the demographic is vastly females and sent out some surveys. It was incredible! I received hundreds of responses. That was it, I knew I needed to proceed with my amazing business idea as it was not just me, it was so many others also.

I started getting my creativity on for a few hours every day after my corporate job, buying fabrics and trim from Spotlight, doing what I believed would bring my business to life. It was simply in my head:

1. Create an idea.
2. Believe in the idea.
3. Pick some fabric and colours.
4. Have a catchy name.
5. Make the product.
6. Launch.
7. Sell, sell, sell.

Reality check: this is not how it works. Starting a business is a minefield, and the idea is just the beginning. You know the saying 'it's about the journey not the destination', well, a business startup is exactly that; it's a journey, and something I know I have learnt and grown so much from over the past nine years. I truly believe the on-the-job education I have received from all my corporate roles and running my two startups, for me, has far outweighed any schooling I could have enrolled in. Plus, it was way tougher as each decision I made had the potential to chew through my cashflow and held me responsible for it all.

It's not that I was new to business. As mentioned, I grew up surrounded by entrepreneurs with both my dad and mum owning their own businesses. I also had a career that saw me work across a variety of industries including automotive, fashion, furniture and bedding, FMCG and pharmaceuticals, and covered all types of sales areas including mass merchants, independent, franchise, retail and wholesale. I knew about sales, numbers, organisations, structures, policies and all the other things in-between, but what I did not know was *how to start my own business* in a nutshell.

Your experience, whatever it is, will come into play and will assist you in many areas. You may not even realise what elements you have taken from previous roles or the influence certain people have provided you with until you start working through your very own business.

In conjunction with your experience, there are all the questions and things you need to think about. But for many, like me, when starting out you don't know what the questions are to ask, so in turn don't know the answers, and it's not until you hit that hurdle or roadblock that you then start thinking about it.

I am not a financial planner or adviser, nor am I a lawyer or legal expert. However, what I do know is what I have been through on the startup journey and what I have learned on the way: the good, the bad and the ugly.

This is what lead me to write this book about business start-ups; there is so much that I now know. I have spent a lot of money learning from my mistakes and am continually educating myself to ensure that I grow my knowledge and can bring new skills to my business that can be used now or in the future.

Now, if you are looking for the book that offers you the 'get rich quick' plan, then this is not the book for you. In writing and sharing my experience and information I've gathered on the journey to date, I wanted to ensure that you hear of examples from my real-life experiences and discover what areas you need to look at in your own business. You may choose to read from cover to cover to really understand my entire journey and then select the chapters that are of interest to you and your business, or you could only read the areas of interest and plan your next moves from there. There is no right or wrong way in business and there is no guaranteed $0 to $1million strategy that will work for everyone, so customise your journey and use the knowledge you gain to work to your advantage.

Your journey will be different to mine, and mine to yours, but having a checklist to assist with areas you need to look deeper into or plans you need to ensure you set your foundations up will enable you to move forward with the best possibility for success.

For me personally, I had a lot of misconceptions as to what I would get from owning a business. Coming from a corporate background where the businesses I worked for had larger teams who managed areas within the business and gave me the support to complete my role, I had not had to wear all the different hats at once. But with my own business, everything fell on me: financials, product design, marketing, administration and buying, sales and legal. This collectively takes us a lot of time and money. I also thought the money would be flying in – I was so passionate about the brand, products and businesses I'd started, so I just believed everyone else would be too. I'd not thought about how long it would take to sell five thousand pairs of underwear or three hundred shisha kits, both of which arrived at my warehouse within days of each other.

Regardless of what was thrown at me daily, I always had passion and a positive attitude that I relied on to keep me going. On the days where I feel defeated or deflated (you'll need to know this because it will happen you), I like to look at the overall scope of what I am doing and see if it really does fulfil me and offer the joy I want from my career.

On the flip side, on the days when it is all happening and life has never been so good, I stop and celebrate the wins. Yes, I still stop and celebrate wins like a $10,000 sales day or signing a large new wholesale client with something specific, like a glass of champagne that night or a special lunch the next day or just a daggy office dance to enjoy the moment.

I also try and acknowledge these because as a small business owner we can tend to just mind our business and keep travelling on. But this is where our drive and energy can really be boosted, from stopping and acknowledging those moments. So please promise me you will celebrate these moments, and if you don't have anyone to celebrate with, message me, I will cheer you on all the way.

Remember to check in to see how you are tracking mentally in your journey. If you chat with anyone in my close circle, they will always talk about how positive I am. I start my day with affirmations and 99% of the time see the glass as being half full not half empty, and I believe that you and your mindset are as a big of a part in this as the business itself. Think about the saying 'you can taste that this was cooked with love' when people talk about food. A business is no different; if the love and passion don't come together with the ingredients, then it's just another business with a product to sell. But if all the ingredients are cultivated together with love and passion, the recipe has the secret ingredient and will always have a better chance of people feeling that warmth. Sometimes, it will be harder to approach the day with a positive mindset. You will feel flat, defeated or just want to give up – this is real, and know we have all been there. I have not met anyone who has not had a bad day and wanted to quit, run away and not look back. That is okay, we are human and are allowed to feel these emotions, so don't get angry with yourself. Validate these emotions and try to not take it personally. Take some time and process how you are feeling. On the days when you only feel 40%, just make sure you put 40% into what you are doing and know that it is your best.

Throughout the chapters, you will see me talking about checking in with yourself to see how you are feeling, as it is natural, as mentioned above, that you may feel overwhelmed with some of the information either from fear of the unknown, the sheer workload or just because everything combined can be a large amount to focus on. Try to not let this deter you, take your time, this journey is not a race and not everything needs to be completed straightaway. The key is to work and grow your business at *your* pace and most importantly keep moving forward in a way that works for you. Do not compare yourself with others as you are not them. Your business and startup is unique to you, so if you keep moving in a forward direction and at your own pace, you are on the right track.

There are some statistics that I want to share with you as I think they need to be known by any new business owner, and they can be scary but worth knowing as there is no one formula that will work for everyone.

It is suggested that over 90% of startups will fail, with 70% failing within the first two to five years, and it's said that the four biggest reasons for failure in startups are:
1. Money is the sole focus, lacking passion.
2. Lack of planning.
3. Lack of marketing knowledge.
4. Lack of perspective of the businesses' potential shortcomings.

These stats can create fear, or they can drive you to be more prepared and in sync with your business, ensuring you truly understand it and stay true to your passion, values and beliefs to give yourself the best chance at being a success story.

There is no right age or time to start your business. Think of stories like Colonel Sanders who did not create KFC until he was in his sixties. Or Mikaila Ulmer, who reportedly went from selling lemonade that was her grandmother's decade-old recipe in front of her Austin home at the age of four, to shipping over 360,000 bottles of Me & the Bees Lemonade to five hundred stores at the age of thirteen. Google states that the average age of a founder today is forty-five years old. So, it's never too early or too late to start; your time is when you are ready.

A lot has changed for me since that moment in 2012, over the past nine years. Knowing what I know now, I personally would not have launched my business, Everyday Lingerie Co, ten weeks after having my son. I would have focused on my website and the key elements of organic traffic over social media more initially, or potentially not even started my business at all. Time and education are amazing, and on reflection, I would have chosen many different ways – in particular, getting to know the financials better and even potentially walking a different path altogether. There are many more examples that I will talk about in the coming chapters. I share this with you because I want to normalise the challenges we can face and ensure you can see how different elements can change the course of your business. The more honestly I share my journey, the greater the knowledge you and others can obtain when building your brand.

My two ecommerce startups could not be more different in terms of categories; however, I've learned that their basic principles are the same. As I've navigated the road through both, I've seen how the foundations and basic structural understanding has helped as business owners to move through the journey more strategically and with clearer directions.

I have often said that if I had known at the beginning what I now know, I could have saved a lot of time and money that was spent unnecessarily. However, the lessons have been great, as I continue to grow and evolve within the businesses and navigate the new normal since March 2020.

Creating a startup is such an incredible experience, and I

have been so grateful to not only be someone who has started a business, but also now begun working with other new business owners to help them on their journey with my one-on-one consulting, something that ultimately lead me to write this book; to offer more people around the world who are thinking about taking the leap, the opportunity to look at my journey and what I have learned and hopefully inspire them to start taking the actions to see if this is what they want to do and help them on that path.

Congratulations for taking the first step as this can be the hardest, as sometimes we can lack self-belief in our own abilities. Sometimes you won't have the support around you in your tribe, but don't let that deter you, if you do the work and add the passion and love to your startup, you'll have the perfect starting point.

I am writing this book for you, as I want you to have examples of real-life areas that I have seen in my journey. To help you see the potential journey ahead through the clearer eyes I wanted when I began. I spent the time completing numerous courses which collectively offered me so much insight along with all the mentors that I have been blessed to have assist and drive me on my journey.

Please remember that this is from my journey and my perspective – others' opinions or techniques may vary, and that is okay, being on a business journey needs to be individual to you and as will your approach, this is about where to start and how to save time and push the opportunities for yourself.

I also learned that there are three ways to complete each part of your business. The first is doing all the work yourself – this can be the most time-consuming approach, but less costly. The second is doing the groundwork and then employing a business or individual to assist with completing an area. This second approach means you need to be a good communicator, understand deadlines and have the funding for the external parties. And lastly, you can completely outsource the business actionables to a professional business or individual who is a specialist in that area. This third approach is similar to you being a project manager, and you must be clear on finding ways to meet all cashflow requirements, but you will have the time available to work through this as most of your other business work will be outsourced. There is no right or wrong way, you need to decide what works for you and how this will financially fit your journey.

Throughout the chapters, I have created a list of tasks for you that you can use to help get areas of your business planned and organised to help minimise wasted time and stress. The more you plan now, the better foundation you'll have to start with.

You will notice that I often talk about visual references in the chapter tips. I am a highly visual person, so for me, vision boards have been a great tool and clarified things for me on many occasions. I still refer to my original boards today when I need to check in.

For those of you who love taking notes, I've got you covered. At the end of each chapter there is a couple of ruled pages for notes, rather than having to go hunting for a pen or paper whilst you're reading, you can simply add any notes or light-bulb moments into this area to ensure you get those golden nuggets written down.

Finally, I want to talk about the 'self-check-in' section for each chapter. This is probably one of the most important tasks

I wanted to add for you. As I mentioned earlier, your mindset and self-checks are super important. Checking in with yourself to see if you are feeling stuck, frustrated or happy to proceed will help you determine when and where you need to ask or look for assistance.

You don't need to do everything yourself, and completing these questions will enable you to see if it's time to get some assistance – and it's okay to ask for help. There are a lot of coaches, consultants, trainers, networking groups and don't forget your personal network to reach out to when you need help, even YouTube and Google are at your fingertips.

Sometimes it's as simple as chatting with someone to get you going again. When I find I hit a block, it is normally because I am overwhelmed and unsure what to take for my next step. When this happens, I either book time with a mentor, family member or friend, and this conversation generally helps to clear the block and set me back off on my way.

So now it's over to you, make sure you have your pen ready so you can take all your notes and jot down the amazing ideas and actions you come up with along the way and enjoy making your journey unique and completely yours.

Danielle xxx

Disclaimer: For financial or legal advice please always find a registered professional that can assist. All numbers or information regarding potential agreements are just examples used within my businesses, please ensure that you seek professional advice for your business, as I always do.

CHAPTER 1

THE GROUNDWORK

'The value of an idea lies in the using of it.' – Thomas Edison

I tried so hard to set off and get my business running as soon as possible, but it quickly became evident that there were a couple of areas I needed to deep dive into to really understand that in order to get my business off the ground, it wasn't just about product.

One of the people that had been my go-to in the early stages told me about someone that was in a similar industry and reached out on my behalf to see if they would help me to deep dive into the potential business idea I had.

I was ecstatic. There was one condition; I had to jump on a plane and head to New Zealand where they would give me an entire day of their time to take me through everything they could. I booked my ticket within twenty minutes of reading the email, and within the coming weeks, I was off for my first trip to New Zealand.

This was the best eight hours on my startup journey I could have ever dreamed of. I remember the excitement as I sat down for the meeting. Wow, I felt like an imposter. All the cockiness I'd had up until this point was gone, and there I was, talking with someone who had not only worked in the lingerie industry heading up a major label, but was also the founder of another one – to me, he was royalty.

I met Stefan and his general manager for lunch first and then we headed to the corporate offices. As it was the weekend, I had the founder's and general manager's full attentions. For the first thirty minutes of the sit-down, I felt like I had 101 questions flying at me: Who are you? What's your career background? Why do you want to start this business? What are you offering? Who are you targeting? When do you want to launch and how are you doing this?

I answered all these questions very quickly, and as notes were written on the board, key things started to be circled. The next words I heard really struck a chord in me: 'You are not strong in marketing or branding – you need to find someone to help in all the areas you don't know, their strength will counteract your weaknesses.'

I had thought that as a startup I needed to do everything myself, and money was always in the back of my mind. This made so much sense. *Shit,* I had been looking at everything the wrong way.

We then continued as I showed what I had currently with designs, names etc. These were all great foundations, but we realised very promptly that I had missed some key factors in my planning. Well, I had not planned it out systematically at all, and

I certainly was not clear on what I was able to bring to the brand to ensure it was set up with a solid foundation.

This was not like me at all. I had grown into a very systematic person and loved planning and have a passion for spreadsheets, but this highlighted to me how I needed to go backwards to really move forwards. I had let the excitement of what I saw take over, and the logic needed to come back into the equation as I was going to try and launch an unknown brand with six to eight designs, each with four colour variants and eight size variants, meaning a bucketload of stock, and for a new-to-market brand, this was way too much, but I had not understood this.

So starting back at the beginning, I went and sat in my seat on the plane on my return flight home and wrote down the six key areas I needed to cover, to really look at my business and figure out how this startup was going to get off the ground:

1. What.
2. Why.
3. Who.
4. When.
5. How.
6. Me.

WHAT am I passionate about? If I am going to be doing this, is it just to earn money? Is this something that I want to be doing every day? There is a vast difference between a hobby and a business, which one did my passion fit into for me? My passion was burning bright for Everyday Lingerie Co, and it was all I thought about. I also wrote down WHAT the brand was.

Everyday Lingerie Co sells everyday underwear that are made

from sustainably sourced bamboo designed for comfort, support and breathability for sizes 8–22.

WHY am I starting this business? Will I be offering a product to people that will make a difference in their lives?

For me personally, Everyday Lingerie Co was started so I could sell Australian-made bamboo underwear that feels like customers are wearing nothing at all. We are focused on promoting self-love within our community. I wanted every person wearing my garments to love the skin they are in so I needed to ensure each product would mould to the wearer and not the other way around. This also meant an ethical factory to work with. This was a large part of the project for me; how could I celebrate a message of self-love and feel like I was enhancing my customers' lives if the garment makers were not being looked after also? This was something that took a lot of time as it was non-negotiable.

WHO am I selling to? What do I know about my target audience? Age, financial status, hobbies and interests? What do they do on the weekends, what do they look for in a brand they buy etc.? Many people or businesses refer to this as your 'target customer' or 'target demographic'. They like to create personas or avatars for this so it's clear for anyone who works in or on the brand.

We have three target markets and three avatars for Everyday Lingerie Co, these are included in our brand style guide (we will talk about creating a brand style guide in a later chapter). This is so I have a very clear picture for all the companies I work with; whether it's building the website, working on social media, crafting ads or developing new products, I always come back to this to ensure I stay within what my customers want.

Creating your target market or customer avatars can easily be pushed aside, however, building these out allows you to be clear and plan for those customers within all facets of the brand and business.

When you understand who you are selling to, you can then expand to be clear on the tone and words that can be used within your communications.

WHEN will I be able to launch? When do I need to get everything completed by? This includes the website, products, processes, packaging, social media accounts, domains and everything in-between.

This is big because you need to work with time lines so you can follow the progress, and almost everything in startups can be entangled into other areas, so knowing dates and planned time lines helps to keep everyone on track. I used a shared Dropbox and created a spreadsheet (for those who know me, that won't come as a surprise – I love spreadsheets for tracking) to have a running list of all the tasks and who was accountable for them, with target dates. You don't have to have this completed from the beginning, but you do need to think about the key areas that you will need to work on and build them out over time to get your business going.

HOW am I launching? Have you thought about this, do you need to start building your audience today?

For me, this meant considering my customers and if I was running just retail online or wholesale too and how I was going to connect with these markets as both have very different requirements.

The best thing about starting a business today is that

marketing is the easiest it has ever been. Back when I started in retail, you either had to pay for ads in catalogues, the yellow pages, local and national newspapers, or you had to set a budget for radio and TV advertising. Today, you have the amazing world of social media at your fingertips. You have access to over one billion people globally just on Instagram alone, with over 70% reportedly being active monthly users. This is a major step forward and huge opportunity for startup businesses.

Every business will need a different strategy in this area. For example, with Everyday Lingerie Co, I can advertise freely across all social media platforms and Google if I follow the guidelines for the images and copyright. However, with Shisha Works, due to the nature of our products, we cannot advertise at all – including boosting posts. These are things you need to think about from day one as you need to communicate with your market to sell products and become a profitable business. What platforms or media can you use within the guidelines?

Finally, ME! What am *I* offering the business? Where do my strengths and capabilities lie?

I am so glad that I received the wake-up call that highlighted to me I don't need to wear every hat and instead I should focus on my areas of strength. This freed up so much time and released so much angst. I didn't need to become a social media guru overnight to propel my brand into the world. Focus on product development, sales, processes and customer service. Find businesses to assist with marketing and branding. I now focus most of my time within the business on product designs, blogs, website and sales. I have spent a large amount of time on education for myself to further my knowledge in my areas of weakness.

Learning more about SEO, marketing, PR and branding has been great for me, whilst I leave the heavy lifting to the experts. But I do also try to ask lots of questions so I can learn and gain understanding which has allowed me to then look at these areas differently and offer strategic and informed ideas to the conversation. I now have a great understanding of actions that I can take to assist in these areas on a daily basis – we will cover this more in the marketing chapter.

ACTIONS

Now it's your turn – grab a piece of paper or something you can take notes on and go over all these areas and fill in what this means for you. Write with as much detail as you can so you can be super clear on your vision and have strong reference points to review throughout your journey.

- What is the business going to offer – product or service?
- Why is this business important, why will your product or service enhance someone's life?
- Who is this targeted towards – ideal customers? Think about customer avatars that you will build on down the road.
- When will you be able to create this with a rough time line?
- How will you be launching?
- Me – what do *you* offer? A SWOT analysis is always a good way to check in and make a clear decision (strengths, weaknesses, opportunities and threats). Play to your strengths and what you enjoy in work so you can bring the best to your business.

You should now have a clearer base plan to consider what your startup will offer and what you need to start researching and actioning to bring it to life. Expand on this with as much detail as you can to ensure that you can fully communicate this with somebody else.

With everything you create along your journey remember that this is a starting point; you will evolve along the path and so will your business. As this happens, update your purpose and key plans to ensure that they are in alignment with your vision and the outcomes you desire.

TIP

If you are finding it hard to complete the above exercise you can always use a vision guide. Creating a vison board for your business can really assist in the process as you gather images like:

- Products that are similar.
- Specific images or pieces of fabric or someone who is in the same service of business you want to offer.
- Images of your ideal customers. Anything that relates to the who, how, when, why, me.

The visual reference can assist with clarifying what you want and act as some inspiration throughout your process.

SELF-CHECK-IN TIME

How are you feeling?

Take the time to check in with yourself every chapter to make sure you are not feeling overwhelmed. If you are, go for a walk or meditate and clear your head, then come back to the exercise and read through it again, and don't put too much pressure on yourself, this doesn't have to be perfect, you just need to start so you can build from here.

I have learned that looking further into my fears or stress points allows me to clarify what I am concerned about. If I allow these pressure points to build, I can become unproductive and waste time, so I look inwards to find the answers.

NOTES

CHAPTER 2

THE MARKET AND HOW YOU WILL STAND OUT

'The value of you and your product or service lies in what you think it's worth, along with the value your consumer sees.'
– Danielle Sady

IT'S TIME FOR MARKET RESEARCH

Getting to know what is happening and who is around you is important. I don't personally like the word competitor. The reason for this is I believe we are all unique and offer something slightly different, but in practise this is traditionally referred to a competitor analysis. My preference is to label it market analysis or market research. I believe we all offer our own unique spin on different products or services based on our experience in life, but understanding what is being offered and how each business is different regardless of if they provide a product or service is extremely necessary.

This is all about seeing how each brand is different and can take quite a bit of time. I completed this for both my startups and looked at a minimum of five to ten businesses in their respective categories in detail, to really understand how our offers would sit next to these other retailers in the market. In doing this exercise, I was reminded about how I needed to be authentic with my brand and focus on what I wanted to do. I was already chatting with some manufacturers to get rough pricing ideas, and all of them kept telling me that I couldn't do bamboo underwear easily and I needed to switch to an organic cotton.

I knew, as I had completed this exercise, that if I changed my concept from bamboo to cotton underwear for Everyday Lingerie Co, I was going to be almost identical to most of the other brands that were already in the market. My cuts would be different, but there were so many people doing this already and they were well-established and doing amazingly. I stood my ground and pushed on, and I am so glad I did because every time I get dressed in the morning or receive a message from my customers talking about how much they love the fabric, and how it feels like they are wearing nothing at all, I know I made the right decision.

Everyday Lingerie Co has never been solely about the underwear; the message the brand carries is always at the top of my mind. The brand came together from a pain point I experienced while shopping to find underwear that I could comfortably wear and go about my day, tackling whatever it brings. My body type was also never reflected in any advertising I saw whilst growing up. Combining these two keys elements into the business was really a no-brainer, and as I completed the market research, I noticed that there was next to no brands that showcased models in different sizes across their range, and if they did, their images were heavily edited. The path moving forward became clearer and clearer for me. I had to ensure that the brand was 100% Photoshop free. Backgrounds could be edited to ensure clear imagery, but the models would not be allowed to be retouched in any way.

Had I not completed this part of the planning, I would never have seen this within the marketplace and would have missed the opportunity to ensure our brand stood out to our followers and customers. Now every customer that chooses to shop with my brand can view the item in the size they are looking for on an everyday model.

If you are creating something completely new to the market, then that's amazing, but there are always other businesses that offer something similar, so really utilise this step.

In the previous chapter you started to uncover who you are wanting to sell to or attract to your business, so now you need to develop the knowledge about how to stand out from the crowd.

Doing this research will uncover a lot of very useful industry information for you.

With your research this is not just about the product, it is also about what these brands or businesses offer.

If they offer physical products, what are their colour options, size range or styles?

Do they have a rewards program or free shipping?

Where do they ship to?

Look at pricing and their social media. How do they interact on these different platforms, how can you see their brand message? What is their engagement like?

Who is their target customer?

You can purchase products to see their full customer experience if that is in your budget, as this will allow you to see product finishes, packaging and any offers they send out to actual customers.

ACTIONS

Create a spreadsheet to complete your market analysis – set up a table and include the following headers in your columns:

- Business name.
- About them. When did they start, anything significant about the biz – reading an 'about us' page on their website will also offer a lot of insight for this.
- Retail or wholesale – or both, for product-based businesses.
- What they offer. Range and sizes or packages.
- Price points or price ranges (if available). Many service-based businesses may not have this available to view.
- Website. How easy is it to shop, what are their key messages, how is the shopping experience, what information can be found on their website, what can you see from their imagery?
- Social media. Look at their accounts. Are they on LinkedIn, TikTok, Instagram, Facebook, Pinterest, Snapchat?
  - List their followers, how often are they posting, what message can you see, their Instagram engagement (the calculation to work this out: divide the total number of likes and comments by the follower count of the account and then multiply by one hundred). I tend to use the last six to twelve posts, then add all the comments and likes together

then divide by the number of posts to get a good average. Example: over twelve posts the account has 1,200 comments and likes. 1,200 / 12 = 100. 100 / 6,000 followers x 100 = 1.66 engagement rate.

- Look at the hashtags they use. Are they the same every time or different? We will talk hashtags later so this will come in handy.

• Look at branding. Colours, tone, imagery etc. You want to ensure that your branding is different and cannot be mistaken for another brand already trading.

• If it's a product:
    - Do they offer free shipping – what dollar value, where to?
    - Do they have a rewards club?
    - Do they offer discounts or packages?

SELF-CHECK-IN TIME

How are you feeling?

Are you feeling excited about completing a market review/ analysis?

Have you already started looking at other brands who offer similar products?

If you are feeling excited, it's time to get started and commence your research.

If you are feeling overwhelmed or stuck, walk away for an hour or so, set a timer if you need. Go for a walk, call a friend to talk about how you're feeling.

Once you feel ready start your research, work on this for as long as you need to ensure you have all the information you require to understand the market. When you're ready, start the next chapter.

NOTES

CHAPTER 3

YOUR UNIQUE
SELLING POSITION

'You are unique and so is your business, so celebrate it.'
– Danielle Sady

Congratulations, you have now worked to understand your brand's groundwork and researched the market. Now it's time to formalise how you are unique with your USP.

The USP is the unique selling point or proposition. These are the features or characteristics of a product or service that are key differences you want to showcase when talking about your business.

This was one of the areas that I found really challenging in both businesses at first, as I have always struggled to articulate the words, so I started by completing bullets points that I could then turn into structured sentences.

Shisha Works example of key features:

• Modern.

- Innovative.
- Ancient tradition.
- Retail and wholesale.

Shisha Works is a retail and wholesale company that imports and distributes innovative shisha products from around the globe that offer a modern twist on an ancient tradition for their customers.

As you can see, once I listed all the words, we could describe the business with them and it became clearer what we were offering and allowed us to bring together a simple and effective statement about who we are.

Some believe this is not important when starting out, however, it sets the tone for everything to come. When we are looking at new products to add to the range, we go back to our USP and see if the new item aligns with it. Most of the time when we have not checked in, we have found that these items have not sold as well as ones that align, and that is because in the past five years our customers have created an ideal of what we offer, and they expect something different, not the standard items, as that is how and why this business was started.

Everyday Lingerie Co was a very similar process.

The keywords we worked with were:

- Comfort.
- Support.
- Breathability.
- Everyday.
- Australian made.

Everyday Lingerie Co design and manufacture premium sustainably sourced bamboo underwear that offers everyday women comfort, support and breathability to allow them to go about their day knowing ELC has them covered in amazing Australian-made underwear.

The USP was updated when we moved our manufacturing from overseas to Australia and yours may also. Allow your brand to evolve over time and grow; I want to encourage you to revisit these statements over the course of founding and scaling your business, so you can have a clear message to refer to.

Do not be worried if it is not perfect. It's a starting point, and you need to begin somewhere. This is also not about you having to publish these sentences, this is about insight and understanding so you can move forward and ensure you align with your brand in all the steps you take. It's a great idea to keep this up somewhere in your office or workspace so you can be reminded of it daily when you work and build your brand to ensure you feel it.

TIP

If you are finding it hard to complete the above exercise, stop and take a moment, write down a few keywords and then create a sentence, read it back and close your eyes. Sit with it, does it feel right to you?

If not, that's okay, you have a few options: call a friend or someone in your network and talk it through with them or write down one or two more ideas. See if either of those feel better. Again, don't panic if they don't, you may need to walk away for a while and come back to this.

Remember there is no right or wrong answer in anything you do, this is your business, and you are in control, so relax and come back to it.

Once you have it finalised, you can now build your elevator pitch.

THE ELEVATOR PITCH

Imagine you have jumped into an elevator and you're heading up to the top floor. Your mentor or ideal business client is in the elevator with you, and you have around thirty seconds to create a connection and get their interest in your product or service – that is what an elevator pitch is.

You never know when someone will ask you about what you do, or you may run into someone you need to communicate your business to at short notice, so I always recommend having this ready from the start.

Some key points are:

1. Introduction – the product or person.
2. Overview – the problem you are solving.
3. Solution to the problem.
4. Benefits you offer.

It really has a beginning, middle (split into two components: the problem and how you solve it) and a conclusion.

With the thirty seconds, you don't want to be talking too quickly as people can find that to be overwhelming or see it as a sign of nerves, which you don't want, so keep the wording slower to showcase you and what you're offering very clearly to whomever you are addressing.

Again, there is no right or wrong with this, just keep checking in with yourself and make sure if feels right. Don't feel pressured by wanting to get this perfect, it took me a week or two to finalise it, and I still change this from time to time when talking to people. I see the written version as the basics but alter the language or spin slightly depending on who my audience is, and this has served me well.

ACTIONS
- Create your business USP.
- Create your elevator pitch.
- Put your USP and elevator pitch up in your workspace so you can refer to these throughout your journey.

SELF-CHECK-IN TIME
How are you feeling?

Are you getting more excited clarifying what your brand is and gaining understanding into the foundations of your business?

If you are feeling excited and smashing through the exercises, that's wonderful, congratulations. If you are finding the groundwork and setting up overwhelming, that is okay too. We all work at our own pace and in our own time.

Look within your network and see if there is someone you can talk to or put the work aside for a day or so, allowing you to relax and clear your mind. Maybe complete a meditation or other self-care exercise that works for you to take a break with.

Remember, there is no right or wrong with any of the work you are doing, you just need to be proud of everything you accomplish.

NOTES

CHAPTER 4

NAME AND REGISTRATION PLEASE

It's time for your business name! My favourite quote when thinking about the pressure of a name is from the movie *Pretty Woman*. Julia Roberts is talking to Richard Gere and he asks what her name is. Julia Roberts' character, Vivian, replies, 'What do you want it to be?'

When deciding on your business name, the world is your oyster, and you can pick whatever you want; however, the importance of what you pick needs to be thought about as it can provide much insight into your business for a customer.

Take the example of parents who spend a lot of time thinking about the name that they will give to their child, or a family who just brought home their new puppy. Sometimes it's simple and easy, other times you need to work through what is right.

I remember spending months looking up names for my son

and the meaning behind them. I wanted to find a name that would match his siblings, along with something that had a strong meaning to both of us as his parents and represented our two families being united.

A business name is similar. It needs to celebrate who you are and what you offer. This is different to a logo. Some businesses use their business name as part of their logo, others choose to use the letters; the choice is yours, so make it count.

When thinking about your business name some of my tips are:

1. How will a customer interpret it, does it showcase what you offer?
2. Is it easy to spell? Remember, many consumers will be searching you online so they need to be able to spell this.
3. Is it easy to pronounce?
4. Can you or do you want to use your own name within it?
5. Can your business grow with this name, or does it limit your offering?
6. Are there any other companies using something similar? You don't want to get confused with someone else as it can decrease your visibility to your audience.
7. Try to avoid hyphens and symbols as this will be harder for domain names.
8. Google words or terms in your category, is there something that you can use for inspiration or ideas?
9. Use a thesaurus to look at alternate words that may work also. Just because one specific word is frequently used in the category doesn't always mean that is the best option for your brand.

With both of my businesses, Google searching played a big part in choosing their names. With some industries being limited in their advertising, the power of the name and the searchable nature of this plays a bigger role. The power of a strong, bold and direct name offers the brand keywords to assist with traffic organically.

Everyday Lingerie Co is quite a long business name, but I knew as the brand grew we could move across to ELC as an initialism if we wanted to. The best part is, it is a key search term for customers who are looking for everyday underwear, so we get an automatic lift for this within Google rankings.

The best way to narrow it down is to create a shortlist and run them by people in your network to gauge their opinions. Remember, this doesn't mean you have to select the one they recommend, this is about research, and hearing others' opinions will sometimes provide great advice, but other times it won't. Consider the story of an international singer, who, in 2021, spoke of her new song that was released after many years away from the charts. The song launched with over twenty-four million streams in the first day. In an article, the singer spoke of how she had shared the new music with some close friends before releasing it, and they gave her lukewarm responses. One mentioned that the singer should keep trying. The lesson I got from this story is that your loved ones can only offer their opinion, and it doesn't mean they are always right.

Once the list of names you have created is complete, I suggest you order them from most to least favourite, as now it's time to check if it's available to build your brand.

The key areas you need to look at are listed below, and this is really an action that needs to be completed collectively to ensure you cover all areas. Put the time aside and sit with your business team or by yourself and research it all initially and then execute.

Start with your government registration of the business name, in Australia this is the ASIC register. You enter the name you are looking for and see if it's available or taken. Try different versions of the selected potential name also, to see if there is another version in your industry that is already trading.

To register a business name in Australia you do need an ABN and there is a fee for the registration, so be aware of this cost and factor it into your cashflow and budget planners. Business names need to be renewed regularly. Be sure you enter up-to-date information as you want to ensure that when the renewals are due you receive the notices and any communication that ASIC needs to send to you regarding the registration.

Congratulations on finalising your business name, now you need to check for all the specific areas you want to register this in:

1. ASIC – as mentioned above.
2. Domain.
3. Social media handles.

DOMAIN NAME

A domain is a registered network address.

Next, you need to check if the domain you would like to use is available. This can be done on any domain provider website. I suggest checking these prior to registering your business name with ASIC or your local authority to ensure that you can have these matching and all aligned for the brand.

There are many different types of domains, and you need to make the call on what suits you:

- .com
- .com.au
- .net
- .net.au
- .shop

Just to name a few – there are literally hundreds of possibilities. In Australia many businesses use the '.com.au' domain and now the '.au' domain, as this highlights to customers that the business is a registered Australian business. There are many differing opinions, the choice is ultimately yours, and as with most of your journey there is no right or wrong.

For example, Everyday Lingerie Co's domain is everydaylingerieco.com. This was purchased once I selected my business name and is the exact same spelling and wording as the brand's business name.

I have around thirty domains registered for my businesses to date, and I chose to do this as I wanted to ensure that if I were to expand, I'd have the option with the other domains already being owned by me, and this also prevents others from registering a similar domain name to mine. As they are a low-cost item, it allows me to keep them there as a just-in-case situation. This is not something everyone chooses to do, however, if you do it's best to factor in these costs from the start.

TIP

I have created a domain registration spreadsheet that lists all the domains with purchase and expiry dates on them, allowing me to track and know when renewals are due.

Knowing the renewal date(s) is important just as with your

business name registration, since your website will be running off this domain and an unpaid renewal could mean no website, in turn causing you to lose sales.

SOCIAL MEDIA HANDLES

I class social media as all the applications that offer me an opportunity to market and champion my product to customers:

- Facebook.
- Instagram.
- TikTok.
- LinkedIn.
- Pinterest.
- Twitter.
- YouTube.

When looking at the different platforms, first list them in order of importance to your brand, you may only use one or you may use all of them.

I have secured all the above for Everyday Lingerie Co so I can confidentially know that another businesses or users can't use my brand's name on any of the platforms. We don't currently utilise TikTok or Twitter, but they are there when we want to explore them.

Registering social media handles is free, it will only cost time for you to set these up and have them available to your business for future use.

TIPS

- Try not to use hyphens or symbols in the handles, including full stops.

- Try to keep all handles identical to your business name.
- Think about how it will be searched on that platform.
- Be aware of the different guidelines across platforms – Everyday Lingerie Co on Facebook is @everydaylco as we had issues with Facebook guidelines on using the word lingerie. Whilst many other companies use that word within their page, we were not able to get this reviewed and it was rejected numerous times, so we settled and found that people are still able to search us easily.

COMPANY STRUCTURE

When it comes to your company structure, I recommend you speak with your accountant and/or legal representation to ensure you make the right decision for your company structure and that what works best in your country. This will include any registrations you will need for tax purposes. These are extremely important as every country has different tax-free thresholds and you need to understand what will be expected of you from the beginning.

Having this structure set up initially will also allow you to claim the business expenses to the business, rather than from personal bank accounts to keep track of your expenditure, so book an appointment with your financial advisor.

Once you have reviewed all the registrations and confirmed with your financial and/or legal representation, you can start acting and securing all the registrations you need and want. Then, it's time to celebrate – you are officially now a brand, congratulations!

ACTIONS

- Speak with your financial advisor and/or lawyer to ensure the business structure is set up correctly.
- Make a checklist for all the business name registrations you are creating.
- Create a list of social media platforms that are applicable to your business.
- Check each platform to see if your business name is available.
- Create an account on your desired platform(s).
- Create a spreadsheet to record all log ins (email and password for reference).

SELF-CHECK-IN TIME

How are you feeling?

Have you finalised your business name? If you have, congratulations, what are you going to do to celebrate this business milestone?

Are you feeling stuck and unsure with how to create your business name? That's okay. You can read on if you want rather than complete the actions now, or you can take some time to go off and do something else for a while and come back when you are ready.

Everyone can feel overwhelmed or unsure at times, do not be discouraged by this. Reach out for some help if you need or take some time to relax and centre yourself again.

NOTES

CHAPTER 5

YOUR BRAND IS MUCH MORE THAN A LOGO

'Your brand is not just a logo, it's all the visual references that make it come to life.' – Danielle Sady

Early on in my journey, I learnt the amazing lesson that my strengths were not branding or marketing, and so I hired a branding and marketing company to assist me on the journey to launch. It was through working with some amazing professionals that I discovered a brand is so much more than just a logo.

When you are ready to start developing the identity of your brand the first step is definitely a mood board.

The reason I start many areas of the business and business plans with visual assets is so I can have a reference point that I can draw on and use for communication.

Have you ever had the experience where you speak with

someone and describe what you want to create or do, and they go off and create something that looks nothing like what you saw in your mind? Building your brand and brand identity is no different, as we all interpret words so differently from each other and that can waste a lot of time for you and the designer in this process.

HOW TO CREATE YOUR BUSINESS MOOD BOARD

Start by looking for inspiration pictures, use the internet or Pinterest, whatever works for you.

Look at colours, do they suit the colours you want to use for your brand?

Look at emotive pictures and ask what it is that you connect with in the image, think about how it resonates with your brand. Look for words, are they describing your product or service, or are they offering insight into the tone or language you want for your brand?

Use a large piece of paper if you like the old-fashioned style, or create a PowerPoint or Pinterest board, whichever suits you. Again, there is no right or wrong way, it is about bringing your visual reference points together so that you or anyone you work with will have a clear understanding of what you want to achieve.

Once you have completed this, sit back and review it.

Does it resonate with you and what you want for your brand?

Does it offer a clear view for others to understand your brand?

If it does, that's great, if you still feel it's not exactly there, keep working on it and develop it further, search for more inspiration.

Remember, it doesn't need to be perfect, this is a starting

point, and like everything in your business, it will grow and evolve the same way your USP and brand statement does.

It is now time, if you haven't started thinking about it already, to consider all the branding aspects that come with creating a new brand:

- Business name.
- Font – style.
- Colour palette.
- Language.
- Tone.
- Logo.

These elements all need to be thought about as a collective.

I have seen many new business owners think, *I just need to get a logo and go from there,* however, the branding can then seem disjointed and not seamless or clear to customers. Creating all your brand assets together allows you to build your website, socials, packaging and overall brand message to customers simply, and the completed look will be cohesive.

If a customer looks for you on social media and your logo is different to your website, they may not recognise you, or vice versa.

When products are shipped to customers, does the packaging have the same branding as your website that they decided to buy from? You want them to identify you with not only the products or services but the brand message – which includes your brand visuals.

Once we decided on the business name and did all the appropriate checks to see that it was available, we set about bringing the brand to life and building the brand assets.

Everyone has a different budget for this area of their business, and you can choose either path, whether that's the DIY journey or hiring a professional. There is no correct answer, this is about your budget and your idea of what is right for you.

IF YOU WANT TO HIRE AN EXPERT

Going down this path, you need to start looking for the branding specialist or graphic designer that is best suited to your business.

Whenever you are looking to work with someone new, especially in a field that you don't have much knowledge in, I suggest you talk to around three possible candidates. The reason for this is you don't know what you don't know, so firstly use the time to ask questions about their experience and try to get to know a little about the contact and their business. This allows you to see what they can offer you for your business based on their skill set and see how your personalities work together.

Every time I am looking to work with a new contact or company within my businesses, I focus as much on how I get along with the possible candidate as I do their skill set. I treat it just like an interview; do you get along well, and do you share the same vision for the brand?

This also applies the other way around, the possible business you want to work with can also see how they feel. This is nothing personal, but when you are developing something that is so personal like your brand, you want to be able to communicate with them if you want to change something and don't want to feel awkward doing so.

Key talking points:

- Ask lots of questions. Take the time to write your questions down and have them on hand for your meeting.
- What does this package/price include?
- What are the payment terms?
- How many changes can be made within the price? Get as much detail around this as possible so the contract is very clear for both parties.
- What will additional hourly rates or changes be charged at?
- What is the time line for the work?

Check that contracts or agreements have everything in writing including ownership of the completed assets.

You don't want to get to the end of the process and find you don't own everything or that the company or individual creating can use your branding assets without your knowledge or approval.

I personally find I prefer to reach out to someone via socials or email initially and book a call to chat with them to really gauge how the relationship would work and then send follow-up emails with all the details that have been discussed to ensure that the conversation is recorded and there is no room for error in the agreement – both parties are covered equally.

TIP

Put everything in writing, and from my experience, pay a deposit on acceptance of a quote with the remainder of the invoice due on completion of the project. Most invoices do state that ownership of work transfers across to the client on final payment. Anything created for your brand should be owned by yourself upon completion of the work and full payment being made.

Please try and avoid 100% payments prior to completion of work as this can lead to issues if both parties are not happy with the final production.

Pricing varies greatly, and this doesn't mean one business is better than the other, they rightly have different pricing structures – stick with your budget and find the best option for you. If you are more flexible with the budget, focus on who best offers what you are after.

GOING DIY

Whilst I worked with an amazing graphic designer and branding specialist to start both businesses, I have now taken over several marketing tasks in-house with the help of Canva, and it has been fantastic.

There are many different programs that can assist you with this process, but as I personally used Canva I wanted to share my experience with you.

Canva is a subscription program that offers a free service, however, if you are wanting to have a one-stop shop for your marketing and branding you will need to look at the paid yearly subscription option (around AU$200 per year) to create a brand kit that you will be able to use for all the assets you create.

Canva not only offers templates for videos, social posts, social stories, logos, posters, flyers and documents, it also allows you to load your colours, fonts and logos into your brand kit so you can create any assets or materials for your business in one place. You can also connect your social accounts and build your marketing planners and schedule posts, which is also great to do especially when you're running solo.

To start with I recommend you sign up to the free account and just have a look through the platform and see how it works and if it suits you. As I mentioned, there are many other platforms that offer similar things, but not having used them I cannot share how they compare.

When creating your logo, think about other logos that appeal to you, they may be on your vision board already: background colours, fonts, size etc.

When picking colours for anything I am working on, I love googling the meanings and associations people have with them – especially with such different customer demographics in each of my businesses, I needed to ensure that the brand would appeal to the correct audience.

Obviously, if I used the peach and navy tones from the Everyday Lingerie Co branding in Shisha Works, I would not be addressing the customer base correctly as it would be targeting a female demographic.

The same can be said for the font styles. In ELC we use two fonts in the logo, one is the heading and the second is the sub-heading or body information, so any communication we use in social media follows the same rules.

The font is like the logo, you can google just about anything, see what different fonts represent. Are you looking for a more traditional font style like a serif or a more modern style like Helvetica? The font needs to tie back into the brand, the brand story and the audience you are addressing. We picked a great font for our logo, but when we created our website the font was a lot harder to read, so we had to find a slightly altered version to ensure customers had a great experience.

If you are building a streetwear brand for kids, the font will be edgier and appealing to that audience versus a florist who would more likely look for something that is classic or romantic in style. Therefore, the groundwork you built earlier is there so you can get a reference point.

Can the logo be easily read? This is about both the font style, colour and size.

Try to remember the key point of a logo is a small design or symbol that can easily identify your product or service and sets the tone of your brand. Great examples are McDonald's, Audi and Apple. If you see any of these three logos you know who the brand is without any words or description.

Will customers identify what the product or service is that you offer?

Where in your business will the logo be used? If you are producing a product, will it still work if the size is decreased? I was working with someone who was able to ensure this was the case as underwear has a small print area so the logo would still be visible once decreased.

How will the colours go if they are on a sign? If you will be putting your logo on a building or shop, how will this work for people and will it last in the elements? I know of a business that had a great logo which printed well for them, but when they placed the signs on their building, the harsh elements faded them in a very short space of time and they needed to not only rebrand to fix this but also spend a large amount of money getting new signs put up.

You may be thinking, *But I am a small startup, I don't need to think about shopfronts or outdoor signage yet*, and that is fine, but for those of you who are thinking of scaling, now is a better time to plan for this rather than later.

TIP

When having your logo and brand assets designed, think about whether this will be digital only or if you need these printed. Printing in Australia is normally completed with CMYK colours and not pantone, this means brand colours should be created from CMYK colours for ease of production.

ACTIONS

- Set your budget for logo and brand asset building.
- Decide how you will be creating your brand assets – DIY or with a graphic designer.
- Print and gather items for your mood board for your branding.
- Create mood boards and key notes for your branding.
- Research graphic designers that you may be able to work with, if you are outsourcing.
- Set up meeting times with graphic designers to talk through requirements and learn about their work and see if your two brands are a good fit.
- Complete research for the best online platform if you want to create the branding yourself.

SELF-CHECK-IN TIME

How are you feeling?

Are you a creative person who is loving bringing your artistic flair into your brand? It can be super exciting to bring the visuals to life to really start seeing the beginning of your brand's physical appearance.

Are you not sure where to start and need to call on some professionals? Look at networking groups on platforms such as Facebook. Put a post out to ask for recommendations for designers if you need. Include in the post as much information about your brand and the work required as possible.

Alternatively, take some time to go and complete some self-care if you are feeling overwhelmed and unsure, this will allow you to clear your mind, and come back when you feel ready.

NOTES

CHAPTER 6

MAKE IT OFFICIAL

'It's better to take your time and set yourself up for success,
rather than rush and make a bad first impression.'
— Danielle Sady

If you have not met with your lawyers and accountants yet, you need to book in an appointment with one or both of them to ensure you are set up for success.

Finding a good accountant to assist with ensuring your business structure works is important.

They can help work out how to run your accounts and ensure you stay on top of all payments, incoming revenue and maintain the overall financial health of your business. It is always best to speak with a professional in this area as they can talk you through a plan that suits you and your financial situation.

If you are registering in Australia, you need to decide if you are registering for GST and then will be submitting a business activity statement (BAS) every quarter.

Business registrations are important and have implications for the owner and the business so it is always best to book an appointment with an expert that can assist you in working through this as they will have the knowledge needed for the country and state your business will be running in.

Talk with your expert about your company structure, including whether you need to be set up as a trust, sole trader and/or corporation so you can collectively work out the details and what they mean for you and how you will run the financials of your business.

ACCOUNTING SOFTWARE

I run both businesses using QuickBooks as I found it best suited my needs. With our online stores running with Shopify, we had the option to select Xero or QuickBooks. The biggest issue I found with both of these options was the stock control. Very early on we realised that neither of these ran between the two systems seamlessly for us. This doesn't mean they won't work for you, but be prepared to search for the right option if you are wanting to control stock quantities.

MYOB, Xero and other accounting software systems are available. Go through each of the possible systems and understand what they offer to see if any will assist you. You'll need to think about payroll, reporting, inventory and all the requirements of your business in order to make your final decision.

These subscriptions normally charge a monthly fee to be used and can bring a solid financial acumen to your business and ease of understanding to your financial position, but if you are not able to afford the monthly fee when starting out, you need to have a strong plan for your financial reporting to ensure you are set up for success.

Some accountants offer clients, who don't have the financial resources for account software programs, Excel templates that they have created to register monthly sales and expenses. This is a great solution but you need to be vigilant about entering all the relevant information regularly to gain a clear understanding of where your business sits.

I paid for training for the online software locally to really gain understanding into the system. I learnt in this process that not everyone understands how different businesses operate, and this caused me a number of issues with my reporting. The more you can research and educate yourself in this area, the better your business accounting will be, ensuring that you have more accurate data to work with and in turn allow you to gain valuable business insight to help with decision-making.

I created daily, weekly and monthly tasks to manage this, but I've also employed a wonderful bookkeeper to manage quarterly BAS submissions and assist when I am unsure with things that pop up in the statements, and then our accountant completes our end-of-year tax returns.

THE DAILY TASKS

- Monitoring all bank feeds.
- Review of all orders that sync across from the website.
  - Check GST code.
  - Check rounding.
  - Invoice totals.
  - Funds allocated to correct inbound accounts for

settlement matching.

- Monitor stock (if applicable) between website and accounting software.

• Attach receipts to payments and allocate to accounts.

This takes me around thirty minutes maximum each day now for each business. Many people have asked why I am still doing this myself rather than outsourcing. I not only understand my business' daily sales and expenses, but I also understand my cashflow. If something happens and a large bill is coming up, I know when to allocate and how to make it work. Many people get overwhelmed by the finances in their business and put it on the backburner or too-hard pile, and the truth is, you are then ultimately flying blind which can create bad outcomes.

If you start with a system and procedure to work through this, even just ten minutes daily, when you get to the end of the month it is far easier and less time-consuming. It also will teach you a lot.

I can now journal and split transactions easily and quickly because I didn't give up or pass it off. Plus, if I'm speaking to an investor or my accountant, I can tell them my numbers almost to the cent. This is all part of a healthy business.

CONTRACTS AND AGREEMENT

Next, find a good lawyer – someone you can work with to help develop any documents like non-disclosure agreements or con-tracts for suppliers or when you need the website policy and terms and conditions completed.

Ensuring that these are relevant to the business and cover you and the business in all areas is crucial, and there are many lawyers that work with small or startup businesses specifically which will be best suited.

When we started out, we didn't know what we didn't know, and the GDPR was an area I was unfamiliar in when we opened. For those who don't know, the GDPR stands for the Gornal Data Protection Legislation. It's a law for the European Union that came into effect on 25 May 2018. This law allows subjects (customers) to have the right to demand access to their personal information and the right to demand that an organisation destroys their personal information. This is in related to businesses offering goods or services to individuals in the EU regardless of whether payment was required or not.

I had no idea how to manage this and ensure that I was compliant with the law as Everyday Lingerie Co is available for sale around the globe. My first call was to my to my lawyer to talk through what information my website was obtaining, along with how we would show this in the company's policies. We had a great chat, and once we reviewed everything, we ensured we had this covered.

I don't want to you stress thinking this is a big deal; this is just an example of items that a lawyer can assist with. In the last five years of business, we have had one customer contact us regarding this, and we easily deleted all their data in line with the laws, because we set this up from the beginning.

There are free legal services offering templates for terms and conditions and privacy policies, which many people use on their ecommerce stores, however, I want to highlight that you may then be opening yourself up to not being completely covered from a legal perspective. You can choose to use these templates and then still run the custom template you have created by your lawyer to ensure that you are completely covered and compliant with all laws. For anyone who is working with products that are consumables, I would suggest working with a lawyer directly as there are many more legal requirements that you need to ensure are fulfilled. Your lawyer may even provide templates and then adjust with you to help reduce the cost of the document creation. Once you have these documents created, they will also help form your FAQs on your website for customers to understand how your business operates clearly and easily.

Contracts are the other key area of your business. Spending the time talking to so many possible suppliers at the start, for me, was not only time-consuming, but sometimes nerve-racking as I was worried that these contacts could talk to others about my ideas or products, so I had an NDA (non-disclosure agreement) created specifically for the business. Anyone I was chatting with that I would be disclosing specific details of the business with was asked to sign and return this prior to commencing work. Some may wonder if this was too much to ask coming from a small startup, but from my view, this was exactly what I needed to do. I had spent so long building and designing my patterns and selecting fabrics that I wanted to ensure I protected every bit of work I had completed. It has served me well and is something you may need to think about or discuss with your lawyer.

Contracts are a key area of your business if you are selling a service, manufacturing a product or working with a suppliers, agents or contractors to build your brand. Contracts are there to ensure that the product or service terms and conditions are outlined and include price, time frame, shipping information and so much more. When you are beginning, it's easy to think it's something small and disregard the need for it, but it is even more important. You want to ensure that both parties are on the same page and all expectations are covered in detail so there is no room for error or grey areas that can be misunderstood by either party.

I learnt this firsthand. I was arranging for my initial website to be created and thought most of the terms and conditions were in the agreement, so I accepted them and paid the deposit required. As I spoke with the company, I learned their interpretation of the completed project was very different to mine. This was an extremely costly mistake, and I was not even trading yet, so this amount (a few thousand dollars) exited my bank account, and I was extremely upset by the entire situation. When I look back now, it was a great lesson (I wish I had learned without the cost), however, I knew moving forward the level of detail I would always work with to ensure that agreements or contracts where clear and precise for all.

You will ultimately decide how best to proceed with vendors, suppliers or other businesses, but always keep agreements documented, and if possible, follow up any detailed calls with an email so that everyone has clarification.

There are so many lawyers in business today that focus on working with newer, smaller and startup business founders by offering more cost-effective legal advice. Networking groups are a great place to connect with these types of business and get recommendations from other startup business owners.

BUSINESS INSURANCE

Insurance is important for all businesses especially if you are wanting to offer a service or product in exchange for a payment.

With product-based business, if you are wanting to supply larger retail groups or mass merchants, many of these organisations will require proof of public liability insurance of up to $20million. This has become standard practice and offers both you and your customer protection from financial exposure.

Start contacting insurance brokers or firms to chat and ask questions. Be prepared to answer a lot of questions about how you will be trading, stock holdings, locations, security etc.

The key areas to look at are:

- Public liability.
- Stock.
- Building.
- Contents.

If you don't have stock, are running from home or have a third party fulfilling stock, this will all need to be covered.

Running from a third-party logistics (3PL) or packing facility, you need to ask about what is covered with your agreement: do you need to have the stock in their warehouse insured or do they cover this?

The next part of setting up a business is opening several accounts, and since you have already formed your basic business plan, you will know that there are certain things you need to think about, which are listed below:

- Payment providers.
- Bank account.
- PayPal.

- Afterpay.
- Zip Pay.
- Poli.
- Credit card facilities.

All of the above payment providers are how you will be accepting money from your clients; you need to ensure they have the options best suited to your business and are set up correctly to ensure transactions can be completed easily and quickly for your clients or customers. Ensure you read *all* the terms and conditions of use. Check that you can use this payment platform or gateway for your product or service as they all have guidelines that need to be adhered to.

There are fees associated with payment providers or payment gateways. Read all the terms and conditions and gain additional financial advice where needed to ensure you understand any annual membership charges or transaction fees you will be liable to pay, along with when payments will be deposited or available for you to transfer to your bank account.

Remember all transaction fees imposed will be added to your costings, so ensure you set pricing correctly.

TIP

Some payment providers will ask that you leave money in your account for a specific time or not make payouts for the transactions you have taken for a period to gain a trading creditability with them, allow for this in your cashflow and understand what the specifics are of this agreement so you are not shocked or financially vulnerable when you commence trading. Think about how this will affect your business in that time period.

ACTIONS

- Contact your financial advisors and lawyer.
- Set up your tax registration so that is applicable to your business and country of trade.
- Set up your business insurance.
- Set up accounts with your applicable payment provider accounts.
- Create notes in your budget and cashflow regarding held payouts from providers.
- Factor costs of merchant fees into your costings to ensure they are registered as a cost of sale.

SELF-CHECK-IN TIME

How are you feeling?

Take the time to check in with yourself every chapter to make sure you are not feeling overwhelmed.

If you are feeling overwhelmed, go for a walk or meditate and clear your head, then come back to the exercise and read through it again, and don't put too much pressure on yourself, this doesn't have to be perfect, you just need to start so you can build from here.

Utilise networking groups that can assist or speak with people in your social and family circle that can help you understand your business structure and how to plan moving forward.

If you are feeling great and moving along with all the actions and business set-up, that's fantastic, keep going.

NOTES

CHAPTER 7

PRODUCT OR SERVICE

Offering a product or service have the same foundations, and both take time to develop.

A SERVICE OFFERING

If you are offering a service, the great news is you do not have to rely on anyone else to build your product and won't need to factor in raw materials or shipping, which helps reduce the set-up costs. But you will need time allocated for the design and creation of the documents and the service.

Start with a plan for this and think about what you need in detail.

- List services, including what is included in detail.
  - Provide as much detail and what the outcome is that you want to achieve.
- Create any templates or materials you will need to complete the service.
  - Scripts can be helpful to help people keep on track

with time management and ensure all questions are answered.

- Think about what your service offers and what information you need to obtain for your clients.
- What contract agreements will need to be completed?
- What email replies will you need to have ready to increase efficiency in your business?
- Are you offering physical documents or templates with your service? These will need to be planned and created in advance to match your branding and be of high quality.

- Website copy.
  - Are you creating this?
  - Have your thought about SEO optimisation in the copy, do you need to find a copywriter to assist in this?
  - Terms and conditions and privacy policy.
  - FAQs.
  - About You page, covering what background you have and what benefit you will add to potential clients or businesses with your service offering.

My initial interaction with every client is a client discovery form. This is emailed to them after we have decided to work together. The form has been designed for the client to provide me with all the relevant information that can enable me to start completing the initial deep dive into their business. I use this form as I complete research into their business and create my list of questions and observations for our initial meeting.

Asking all these questions prior to our sessions also gives the client an opportunity to look at their business through a different set of eyes; often clients see things they have not noticed prior, and they can start thinking about how they can change, pivot or alter certain things within their business.

This was all set up prior to working with my first client to ensure that I knew a considerable amount of information that was not too detailed but enough to get the conversation flowing.

Writing my book was no different. I started with an idea, built a plan around all the key areas that needed to be talked about and then I broke it down in chapters. Each chapter has a page of notes with key topics that needed to be covered, then I started writing each chapter. As the chapters were written I built them out further from the discussion points. I was able to stay on track in each chapter and ensure that the details related to the topic at hand.

Once you create your offer, you need to monetise it.

1. How much time will the service take?
2. What costs need to be factored in?
   a. Do you rent an office?
   b. Do you have merchant fees?
3. What additional materials need to be created that are included in the service fee – if you offer booklets, packs or other materials, you need to factor these into your fees.

Every business that offers a service can charge what they choose, there are opportunities to see the industry averages from the market analysis you completed in the actions in previous chapters.

Think of a lawyer as an example. There are different specialities along with different levels of knowledge and positions that warrant different fees. A Queen's Council is more costly per hour than many other lawyers.

If your pricing is set at a higher rate, this will then alter the client or target market that you will be engaging with as it may exclude certain clients – but this is not necessarily a bad thing. Your experience and offers will guide you with how to set your rates.

Pricing and rates can and will adjust over time. For some you will start at a lower rate and grow over time as you feel your experience grows.

As mentioned earlier, I love spirituality and the power of the mind, and many of the books I read or listen to are focused on the mindset individuals have and how these can hold us back at times. There is a great book by Denise Duffield-Thomas called *Get Rich, Lucky Bitch!* where Denise talks about how to figure out what your pricing should be.

The exercise Denise has created asks you to sit with yourself and come up with an hourly rate and then see how that number sits with you. Do you feel like it scares you? Do you feel comfortable with the number? This guide gives you an insight to allow you to find your number that is comfortable and safe to allow you to start from there and build the confidence and mindset that you deserve this, as often we hold ourselves back, believing we are not worthy. If you enjoy these practices, it's a great read and very insightful to help build confidence.

I know you may not be interested in this technique and prefer to use your knowledge and industry experience to create your pricing strategy, but whichever way you choose, go with it and map out the entire plan and packages so you are 100% confident and can stand behind it.

A PRODUCT-BASED BUSINESS

When selling products in your business there are two options to select from: products you purchase that are complete or products you create from scratch. They have similar costing models but are different in how you decide on ranges.

COMPLETED PRODUCTS PURCHASED

This option can be seen as the easier of the two models. Simply source the stock, connect with a supplier, place an order, pay, ship stock and you are ready to go.

It is a great option, and with the internet you can easily start searching for the products you want. Many people worldwide have had great results with their businesses. Just be clear, with this path you need to ensure you have contracts in place and are prepared if things do not go to plan.

To date, we have sourced products from manufacturers in China, Turkey, Germany, Russia, the USA, Brazil and India. Nine times out of ten there have been no issues, but the one in ten where things were not right were frustrating. This can happen, but if you have agreements in place you will minimise the risk.

We have run the business from day one with a specific internal policy and that is that we always purchase a sample piece prior to working with any manufacturer. The reason for this is so we can check the way the stock is packaged, how it's transported, how quickly the supplier dispatches, the overall product quality and how fit for purpose it is.

With this policy we have turned down more suppliers than we have ever stocked. We learnt that viewing an image on the internet and having a physical product in our hands are two very different things.

When contacting a supplier, be sure that you contact them via email (using an email that is associated with your domain name is always a plus rather than a random Gmail or Hotmail) or your social media page so they can be assured you are a genuine customer. Include specific information about the products you are after. If possible, take screenshots and note product codes if applicable. Most suppliers will happily supply samples at a fee.

TIP

I tend to ask, in writing, if any sample costs can be deducted from a final order if I go ahead. You don't know if you do not ask.

Once you have this all organised, order a minimum of one per style or size depending on what product you are looking for and review them in detail.

If it is a garment, check all stitching, seams, finishes of the fabric, how it washes, how it holds up after drying. What are the care conditions that the supplier recommends?

Check the product and try using the product all the ways that it is intended to ensure that it is fit for purpose.

Every sample that arrives at my warehouse is tagged with a swing tag, I note the supplier name, product name and code and the date it arrived. This allows me to track everything so I'll know exactly where the item came from if I ever need to go back and reference it for any reason.

If you are happy with the products, it is time to start working on your buying terms with the supplier.

Key questions to ask:

1. What is the price per unit?
2. What is the minimum order quantity (MOQ)?
3. What is the ETA for them to dispatch the order?
4. Does the cost include shipping?
   a. Is shipping FOB, EX Works – these cost different amounts and need to be covered before any money is exchanged.
5. What are the payment terms?
6. If you have any specific requirements like adding a logo, confirm this can be completed.

Before placing an order, you now need to ensure that your costings work and that you can range this product. The next chapter covers this in detail: how to work out final costs and sell prices.

As a general rule of thumb, the maximum we would pay for an order is a 50% deposit and the balance is payable on advice that the order is ready to be dispatched. Even with companies we have worked with for years, we await the advice that the stock is ready and receive the cargo dimensions before we make the final payment and have our carrier arrange collection or complete the booking for the relevant shipping.

With smaller orders your supplier may be able to arrange shipping via DHL or another air freight provider and include this in the final price. This is really helpful if you are starting out rather than paying an agent fee and can be a lot quicker for the transport.

There are also many recourses that can assist with your sourcing such as: Alibaba, local product shows or exhibits, local makers that can be found via Google searches.

Be warned, beacuse I, and people I know, have had experiences where a supplier has sent samples and the stock looked great and was signed off, but the orders that arrived were not the same as the samples supplied – this is why contracts need to be in place and binding to ensure that these situations are minimised and hopefully never arise.

MAKING YOUR OWN PRODUCT

This is a fun and challenging thing to do. I loved the process, but at times found it really frustrating as I did not have all the knowledge I needed to initially complete the process.

1. Design your product – get drawings done either by yourself or someone in the graphic design area so the product is clearly visible. This ensures that anyone you talk with can share the clear vision you have and lessens the chance of misinterpretation.

2. Start sourcing the raw materials you need. Buying samples of the raw materials allows you to now have something for the makers to physically touch along with your drawings from step 1.

3. Get a pattern and/or CAD drawing with all measurements completed to show all detail. Included in this should be a full tech pack that shows the items' measurements so you have the fabrics, measurements and drawings depicting the final product.

4. Source sample makers for your relevant field. This can be locally or internationally. If you source a sample maker locally you will save considerable amounts of time sending and receiving garments. On average, a piece from China to

Australia can take four to six months plus production time. This will also give you an opportunity to start building your network within your relevant industry if you don't already have one.

5. Review all samples in detail and see how they work with their desired purpose.

6. Finalise the samples if you have not done so already.

7. Sign off on pattern pieces so you can go to production. All product sizes should be finalised in your tech packs, CAD drawings and spec sheets.

8. Source a maker and cover all the key questions with them. Key questions to ask:

• What is the price per unit?

• What is the minimum order quantity (MOQ)?

• What is the ETA for them to dispatch the order?

• Does the cost include shipping?

  – Is shipping FOB, EX Works – these cost different amounts and need to be covered before any money is exchanged.

• What are the payment terms?

• If you have any specific requirements like adding a logo, confirm this can be completed.

9. Work out all costings for your product to check profitability – detailed in the next chapter.

10. Sign off on contract and pay deposit.

11. Receive goods and prepare for sale.

It took over two years to find the initial factory for Everyday Lingerie Co because we had some important brand values we wanted to ensure we covered, which included having an ethical factory. These are things you need to think about when you are sourcing a potential factory.

Are there any brand values that you need to cover with your factory?

If you are working with children's products there are important guidelines that need to be met and adhered to for safety reasons, so please ensure that you research these or talk with your legal representative to ensure you are covering all the laws and legislation correctly.

Whether you source premade product or design and manufacture your own, think about the evolution of the product and how this will grow with the business as the business evolves.

ACTIONS

- Plan out your range of products.
  - What is the total quantity you can and want to purchase – MOQs.
  - What budget have you planned per item?
  - How will your product be shipped from the supplier – locally or abroad?
  - Think about shipping costs and payable taxes upon landing goods from international suppliers.
  - Check terms and conditions with potential suppliers for payments, supply and shipping.

SELF-CHECK-IN TIME

How are you feeling?

If you are feeling stuck, start researching product suppliers or reach out within networking groups to talk with people who have completed a similar startup model, ask questions and see if they can help with queries you have.

Are you feeling great and super pumped about building your portfolio? Amazing, that's great to hear, keep going. Build out the work you want to achieve in the next week to help keep you on track.

Remember it is okay to work through everything within your business slowly and at a pace that you are comfortable with, it is not a race. As the saying goes, don't try and eat an elephant in one sitting, just have one piece at a time.

You've got this, take some time for yourself if you need it. Mediation, a nap or a walk can always help clear your mind.

NOTES

CHAPTER 8

THE DOLLARS AND CENTS

'Pricing your product needs to be right from the start to ensure you are set up for success.' – Danielle Sady

There are three main areas in your business: the product, the brand and the money. All three are equally important, however, if you don't know the cost of your products in detail and ensure all the running costs are factored into the business, you run the risk of not generating a profit and in turn struggling with cashflow from the beginning.

Cashflow is about two key points: the cost of the product to you and selling to the customer and ensuring the margin is there for sales and events ensuring that in every case you make money, and then about scaling and building.

You can choose several structures in your business:
- B2C – Business-to-consumer sales, meaning retail sales only.
- B2B – Business-to-business sales, meaning wholesale only.

Or you can offer both. Whichever option you select for your business, the numbers need to add up.

Retail-only structure means you will sell direct to the end consumer only; you won't be selling into other businesses (wholesale) who then on sell to the end user.

With this structure, if you are selling a service, you will provide the customer the offer online or in person, however, if you are selling a product you need to think about:

- The product shipping – how will you package the item to be shipped or handed to a consumer in store?
- The customer experience – what will the customer see and feel when they receive their package?

These things come at a cost, and that needs to be factored in with the cost of goods when working your retail pricing.

If you are choosing to retail and wholesale, you need to factor in the wholesalers' margins when you set your retails. Please note that you can offer any wholesale customer the recommended retail pricing, but you cannot set the price.

A general rule of thumb with wholesale is that they would want to offer 100% mark-up on all items. For example, if a retailer buys an item for $50, they would intend to sell it for $100. Whilst this example is not set for every category, generally it is a good guide to follow when looking at how to make the structure work within your business or if it is even viable. Please note that the example above does not include any taxes payable, these are purely examples.

First you need to work out the total cost of an item you will be selling, and to do this you need to factor in all the associated costs.

Costs to be factored into pricing are:

- Cost of the product.
- Shipping the product to you or your warehouse from the supplier.
- Packaging costs to ship to the customer.
  - Postage satchel/box.
  - Postage label.
  - Wrapping paper or box that the item is put in.
  - Paperwork included with the item if not already factored into the product cost.
  - Free shipping – if you are paying for shipping you need to know the average cost to add this in.
- Merchant fees – as spoken about earlier, your fees charged by your payment providers need to be added into the goods cost as this will be payable by you with every sale.
- Time to pack an order.
- Time to make the goods if you hand-make your items.

Calculating time to pack an item is important as many don't factor in their time to physically pack and then miscalculate the actual cost. You may start by packing the goods yourself and think that this is not important, however, as you scale your business and start employing people or hire a 3PL to pack the goods, there is a cost associated with this and it is better to have included this earlier rather than later and realise that your profits are eaten away by something you did not think about.

To calculate, use your hourly rate. Use this example with a $30 hourly rate divide by 60 minutes = 50c per minute. Takes 6 minutes to complete the packaging = $3 per package.

If you offer free shipping, this may affect this final number as shipping can cost anywhere from $5 up depending on the service and country it is being shipped to. Look into the options available and see what is viable for you. If you need to start with only local free shipping, start there and build where you can. You do not need to offer free shipping or anything else within your business, but whatever is included needs to be factored into the costings.

Many freights or shipping services offer greater discounts the more shipments that are sent so your costs will hopefully decrease, allowing you to open this offering as you build your business.

I offer free shipping with minimum spends within my businesses as I saw this was an offer across the market upon completing the business analysis. This has all been costed out very specifically for my businesses. As I mentioned earlier, I am a massive fan of spreadsheets, the reason for this is that once I have them set up with the formulas I need, I can alter the data that changes, and everything calculates quickly and easily.

With the recent pandemic, I have seen my shipping costs climb due to new surcharges even though my volume of shipping increased; however, once I received the updated international rates from my provider I spent around twenty minutes entering the new costs, checked the calculations (always good to randomly check two to five to make sure nothing has changed in the formulas) and then updated my price book with the new costs and reviewed all ten regions internationally to confirm they are still able to be provided. In total I spent less than forty minutes from start to finish because I have set myself up for success from the beginning.

Initially when I looked at the shipping costs for the international market, I thought I would never understand it, but it is quite easy once you break it down. If you are unsure, speak with a consultant or sales team member from your selected providers to help you understand the calculations so you can ensure that you get it right from the start.

You will also need to know the weights and approximate dimensions of your products to work out shipping costs – once you have this you can use the calculations to quickly build a shipping cost sheet.

For all my product pricing I have created what I call pricing books that are all in Excel and have been set up specifically for my business and can be easily created for any business. Every supplier or range has its own tab, and they all run off a similar template.

As some products are internationally supplied and some local, they all have an exchange rate built in that will allow me to always start the work with the supplier's currency.

Once I enter the cost in the desired currency, the spreadsheet then does the work, calculating the cost in AUD, then it adds a shipping cost.

International shipping varies greatly depending on size, weight and transport. You will start to see patterns and then be able to have a rough idea of what the average percentage of cost is for your freight as you commence. The cost in AUD then adds itself to the shipping cost, and I then see an approximate landed cost for the item.

From there I enter the retail price I would like to sell the product for. The preset formulas then calculate my average merchant and website fees, as they are charged on the retail cost now, and I can see the potential profit for that item. You will see is it too high? Too low? Just right?

There is no right or wrong with pricing, you are the only one that can judge this. If other retailers are selling a similar or identical product for around $20 retail, I would suggest you are also selling around that same number, not at $50 because you will price yourself out of the market – but if your product is not offered by anyone else you choose the value for your item.

When you are offering packs, there are multiple items to include, but the breakdown for cost calculation is the same and I always use a specific spreadsheet for each pack. This would then have each item on a separate line, which calculates out to give you a total, then you enter the retail pricing as per above.

You want to make sure with any packaging you are using to wrap your products to send out to customers, keep the numbers relative. The packaging on a $1,000 item will always cost more than a $50 item, so factor this in. We all want our package to make a statement to a customer when it arrives, however, it needs to come in at a responsible price that is relative to the product you are supplying and minimise your time to pack.

As mentioned earlier, when thinking about the costs associated with packaging and shipping you need to include:

- The box, bag or wrapping paper the items are shipped in.
- The outer satchel the item is shipped in.
- The postage labels.
- Any cards or offers that are included – handwritten or printed.
- Time to pack.
- Signature for items if you are having your postal carrier add this service.
- Postal insurance if needed.

Each of these items cost your business and need to be factored in. The best example of this is if you think of a lasagne that you buy premade from a supermarket. Every time you buy this item from the same brand the item will be identical and that is because they have costed out the ingredients to ensure that every item is the same and they can be profitable – you and your business are no different to the formula the lasagne company uses.

In Shisha Works, the items shipped are larger, fragile items that take around four metres of bubble wrap to ensure they are secure for shipping. The cost of the bubble wrap is around $15 per twenty-five metres (cost is 60c per metre), so we have factored in $2.40 per item in the shipping costs for the bubble wrap. Having this also allows us to reduce our costs for exchanges or returns of damaged goods and ensures that we are selling an item with profit.

Many business owners often have questions about what to do if you have a parcel that is lost or reported not delivered. These are real things that can happen in business, and without costing this into part of your plan and policies, you won't know how to handle it and can easily get frazzled with how to deal with the customer.

We cover this more in the upcoming chapter about policies and procedures, however, you need to learn what costs of protection you can get for shipping with your carrier, and if you want to select these for your services, now is the time to start costing these options into pricing.

Two examples I personally saw of people struggling with costings are:

- A client once came to me with a product that she wanted to sell for $8.50, she had beautiful packaging the item would be shipped in and she wanted to offer free shipping. We ran the numbers, and the client was shocked to see that not only did the item cost her $8.50, but the packaging cost was $12 and the postage would cost around $8. At this rate she would be paying the customer close to $20 to buy her products.

- Another client was doing well in business making $6 from a low-cost item they sold. When we reviewed the sales and costing, I noticed that they had not allowed for the shipping that it took for them to receive the stock and they had not allowed for the running or merchants fees that were part of their business. Over 64% of their customers were purchasing on PayPal or Zip Pay so in conjunction with 2% retail being a fee payable to the website host they had up to 6% of fees they had not factored in. They were making a loss on this item.

These avoidable mistakes can be managed by setting up your costings before you commence trading. There are multiple ways to track and plan your costs out, just because I love Excel and find this the best solution for me doesn't mean it will work that way for everyone. Regardless of if you want to be the next Sara Blakely (founder of Spanx) bringing in over a billion dollars, or just bring in enough revenue to have a small income, the principles are the same and to plan and be prepared is the key to success, especially with your numbers.

Start today, don't wait until you grow or until the end of the month. The earlier you start, the less confusion and greater knowledge you will have in this area of your business, and setting yourself up for success is the key.

WHAT TO DO WHEN YOU WANT TO RUN A SALE

Have you thought about the sales you are going to run in your business on products?

There are so many options:

- % off sale.
- $ off sale.
- 2 for 1 sale.
- Free shipping.
- Buy *x* get *y* free sale.

There are so many options, and it's great to be unique and run sales when you want. We don't run sales often as we have offered all our products as everyday low pricing to give the customer great value, however, we have still calculated the different sales we can offer when we want to run these incentives.

All sales plans need to be costed out so you know the profits available and how it works. If you are running a 2 for 1 deal for example: Cost is $50 per unit. Sale price is $80 per unit.

Two items for $80 for the customer that cost you $50 x 2 = no profit, that offer won't work.

As I have my pricing books set up for both businesses, whenever I am looking at new items to range, I can make an informed decision in about five minutes if a product will or won't work financially. The power of streamlining your business means you won't be bogged down or wasting time on simple tasks that you can complete quickly and move on from.

ACTIONS

- Create costing book(s) for retail and/or wholesale with price calculators for local or international sourcing. Include:

- Shipping costs from suppliers to you.
- Shipping costs to customers (including cost of packaging materials and time it takes to prepare items for shipping).
- Merchant fees.

• For goods being shipped – plan out what level of insurance or protection you will be prepared to include in your costs, if any.

If you are not confident in being able to create these pricing sheets or books, speak with your accountant, network or a consultant who specialises in these to help get the templates set and get you on your way.

Remember, you don't need to do everything yourself and an external party can assist with your education to ensure you have the tools and knowledge to move forward.

SELF-CHECK-IN TIME

How are you feeling?

Do you love your numbers?

Are you comfortable with creating your costings spreadsheet to ensure you are financially set up for success within your business?

If you are not comfortable, it may be time to ask for help. Reach out amongst your networking group, family or friends to people that may be able to assist with getting this sorted. We are all not comfortable or strong in every area of our business, you have got this – ask for help where you need it.

Remember, you have plenty of time to work towards your goal, there is no need to complete every task today. And enjoy the process of bringing your brand to life, not everyone will ever do this and your journey is unique and special. Soak in all the moments along the way so you can look back with a smile.

NOTES

CHAPTER 9

STOCK
MANAGEMENT

*'Start small and build, more options doesn't always mean
more revenue.' – Danielle Sady*

You have spent the time running your numbers and had them
checked by a financial expert if needed, and now you are ready
to place your order(s) for your stock.

I struggled with this initially – how many in each size, what
colours. It was a constant thought for about ten days. I was
scared, was I making the wrong decision? How do I know when
I haven't sold a piece?

Everyone kept saying the same thing: it's all about forecasting.
But how do I forecast for something when I have no analytics?
It was on day ten that I received a fantastic suggestion to go and
chat with a family friend who owns a 3PL. They range hundreds
of brands from an extensive range of manufacturers. I called and
booked a meeting and two days later I was sitting in their office

feeling immensely relieved.

I explained my dilemma: I was unsure how to select the quantity by size for manufacturing as I had no sales history, and I was concerned on how to divide the MOQ between the eight sizes. It was explained to me very simply: you can have either of the follow ratios:

Size	8	10	12	14	16	18	20	22
Option one	1	1	1	1	1	1	1	1
Option two	1	1	2	2	2	2	1	1

Option one implied that I purchase an equal number of pieces in each size.

For example, with an MOQ of 1,000 units divided by 8 sizes I would look at buying 125 units per size.

This would then allow me to see the results of what customers want once results are starting to filter in.

Option two implied I purchase double the amount of stock for sizes 12, 14, 16 and 18, and half the amount for sizes 8, 10, 20 and 22.

For every one unit I ordered in size 8, size 12 would get two. This tiered option two felt like the better one as on average sizes 12–18 seemed to be moving in women's fashion and underwear, from their knowledge. I ended up choosing this and it was right and wrong. We found out quickly that we didn't have enough size 20 and 22 briefs but were trading well in the mid-range sizes.

The data was finally there to see how our customers were shopping and the sizing was equal across the board. The moral of the story is, you will decide what works best for you once you have the data, you will adjust and work through what works well and what doesn't and change what you need to. Hopefully you get it right from the get-go, but if you don't that's okay, you just need to use the data to assist or your network to work through this.

I was told early on that on average I would have around 25–30% of stock that would either be damaged, lost in transit or not sell, and I needed to be prepared for this, so we factored in sales and events to assist with moving slow-moving stock – some food for thought.

The next steps to think about are how you will manage your stock.

ARE YOU ABLE TO WAREHOUSE AT HOME?

The pros are you have access when you need it and it's the most cost-effective option. Having your stock at home, you will be able to pick and pack at a time that suits you, you don't need to operate in the conventional nine-to-five hours. The disadvantage is you don't have any space away from your business and you can find the business taking over your home and every waking thought as you get no break. Will it mean that you no longer have a garage? How does this work for your insurance? All these factors need to be thought about and whoever you live with needs to be involved to ensure your home life is not completely disrupted. Remember we all need to work on balance.

STORAGE FACILITIES

Do you need to invest in a storage facility that will allow you to pick and pack from there? This option has been used by many businesses and one I did look at numerous times to minimise overheads, but I did not personally feel this would work as my volume was quite large. I decided I needed to store. The cons in my circumstance outweighed the pros for me. Ensure you check the terms and conditions of the facility when looking, including access hours to ensure this works in your needs.

IS A 3PL THE BEST OPTION FOR YOUR BUSINESS?

Overall, there are pros and cons for every option. You need to work through all the options and what suits your business, budget and functionality.

Working through how to manage your stock, costings, low stock alerts and errors with customer orders are all details that need to be handled in your contract with the 3PL.

When working with 3PLs, there are companies that are now working solely with startup ecommerce traders, so they are a lower-cost option as opposed to the traditional larger format businesses. When talking with potential 3PL or shipping facilities, cover all the questions regarding customer service for your customers and ensure the brand is represented inline with your requirements, along with stock levels and insurances for your products. Some facilities may look cheaper, but you may need to pay for additional costs which could end up being more costly per unit. If you are entering a contract, as always, get your legal representative to check over and ensure that all the terms and conditions are covered and understood.

CREATING STOCK CODES FOR IDENTIFICATION – SKU CODES

SKU (pronounced *skew*) means a stock keeping unit; this is the term that allows businesses to identify and track inventory.

Prior to your stock arriving, you need to create SKU system to assist in managing your range. This allows you to have a secondary reference point for the units you are selling which allows for cross-checking when packing – and these are different to barcodes.

As always, a systematic approach is best.

There are 101 ways to run this, and again, it is whatever suits best; no one certain way is best. For example, stock we import in our business from a specific brand that we will be advertising is set up as follows:

EXAMPLES	Brand in letters or numbers or a combination of the 2 for the first 3-5	Style	Colour
3 factors	MREDS/AW100/61000	0001	BLK
3 factors	MREDS/AW100/61000	0001	100
2 factors	MREDS/AW100/6100	0001	No colour code

How these three style code plans work is that I start the brand with letters representing their name then add a style code. Starting with three zeros first and I build from there.

If you want to have codes for colours, you need to create this as a list so you have a solid reference to ensure the same numbers are used across all SKUs.

Most larger businesses use something like example two, varying the beginning to show only the number or their version of style identification and add a size to the end like 008 or 010. If you are creating a brand with small, medium and large sizes, consider how that would also translate across to a number or alphabetical code depending on what you want. Some businesses suggest using seasons for the codes: AW for autumn winter collections or SS for summer and spring.

You can see whichever avenue you take there is no right or wrong, like all the areas in this book, but these are guides to help you think about this area, and again, set you up for success from the beginning.

Creating a spreadsheet or record of how you plan to create SKU codes will assist with all additional lines that are introduced in the future and offer a clear reference point for everyone involved in the business.

BARCODE CREATION

Barcodes are different to SKU codes. If you are selling a product to retailers, many will want you to have this set up already, especially the major retailers as their business are all IT savvy and will need you to be prepared for this. Barcodes can act as a pick and pack tool; you can use a scanner to check orders being packed or sold through your storefront if you have one.

How many barcodes do you need?

If you have one style of product in three colours, you will need three barcodes as every colour must have its own unique barcode. If you have a pair of shorts that is in three colours and ranges in three sizes (small, medium and large) you will need 3 x 3 for a total of nine barcodes.

There are six different types of barcodes, and the type you

need depends on your business. For stock items, such as what I carry, I purchased EAN-13 barcodes as these are used worldwide and work for my needs. However, if you are writing a book or magazine you need either an ISBN barcode or ISSN magazine barcode.

The most useful website I found which was also economical in cost was **barcodesaustralia.com** The team was super helpful and had everything sorted for me so quickly and they also assisted with creating QR codes for our businesses. Once I received all the files, which happened within minutes of our purchases, all were print-ready and easy to add into the Shopify store product records and send off to the printers to have stickers made that were easily added to the swing tags on each garment.

I had been putting off this task as I was so unsure, but through reaching out to a professional company, it took all the angst away and allowed me to action what I needed and learn super quickly. As with everything new I need to action, I did reach out to a few companies and found that some charge yearly fees for the barcode registration. This was going to be costly for a small business – it was through the wonderful world of Google that I found Barcodes Australia, as mentioned, who made the process simple and cost-effective for my business. Do research relevant to your state or country of trade and the laws with barcodes there to ensure you find the cost-effective way to action for your brand.

TIP

If you are printing swing tags, labels or packaging for your product, complete the work in this area before final artwork is completed as it makes it a lot easier to get the artwork completed with everything on it from the start, especially if you have MOQs for the printing. This way you won't have to spend time adding stickers later which takes time and costs more to have printed separately.

ACTIONS
- Create your SKU plan.
- Factor in variations for your products.
- Complete barcode plan and research.

SELF-CHECK-IN TIME
How are you feeling?

Take the time to check in with yourself. Are you finding you are excited about everything you are completing for your new venture? You are now almost halfway through this book and may have had some amazingly big moments happen if you are working through each chapter.

If you find you are overwhelmed, confused or tired, listen to your body and take time out for yourself. Rome was not built in a day, and your business won't be either.

Take some time to acknowledge how far you have come in your business planning and make sure you are celebrating all the wins and accomplishments along the way.

If you are feeling fatigued, ensure that you do something for you, it could be spending time with family, going for a walk along the beach, meditation, reading a book or just dancing around the house to your favourite song. You have got this, just keep believing.

NOTES

CHAPTER 10

YOUR WEBSITE AND FIRST IMPRESSION

'Ecommerce has seen ten years of growth in three months.'
— Tobi Lutke, CEO & founder of Shopify (posted at the start
of the pandemic, 2021)

It's reported that a shopper today has anywhere between six to twelve interactions with a brand prior to buying, so your first impression counts.

Like all areas of your business, websites need planning and a strategic approach. This chapter is one of the largest in the book as there is so much that goes into a great website. Which, if you are like me, you will have no idea about when getting started.

Before I started my brand, I believed I knew what I needed for my website and employed someone to action it, which ended up costing thousands of dollars – a price I believed was reasonable at the time for such a custom website.

I had signed up for a website that was going to offer me a lot of what I needed, but I was locked into working with one specific organisation as it was custom-built on a platform that most people are not trained in, so if I had an issue I would have to use this company, and they were going to be charging a few hundred dollars every call up. Plus I would need to monitor the website for issues and submit requests that would be answered in two to five business days.

Imagine my horror when I found this out. I was so annoyed at myself but decided to finally accept this was not going to work and write it off as a very expensive lesson.

With a website or ecommerce business, you are open to potential customer interactions twenty-four seven, how could I not have support from our developer in a timely fashion?

After my first failed website experience I began researching and started learning about what options I had available to me and what would work best for my businesses.

First you need to know what you are offering.

Below is my summary of what I see works for different offerings:

- Ecommerce (selling items): Shopify or WordPress, and some larger organisations work with Magento.
- Service-based: WordPress, Squarespace (you can also add shopping carts to this platform) and Webflow.
- Membership or education platforms: Squarespace, Kajabi and WordPress.

All the platforms have their space in the market and work for different reasons, and all will function and offer you what you need, but creating a plan or business means an outline and budget that will help you start your search and find how suited each platform is to your business needs.

I went with Shopify and found this to be exceptional for my businesses.

To sum up Shopify, as quoted by *The Cut* co-founder, Ben, 'Shopify is simple, secure, intuitive, robust, along with being flexible and scalable.'

There are many recognisable brands that use Shopify that you may not even be aware of, including Heinz, Red Bull, Nescafé, Lady Gaga, Gymshark, Taylor Swift and Victoria Beckham Beauty.

The platform is easy to use and has a lot of features built in, with the options of apps to customise your website without large amounts of code. As always, the choice you need to make will come after you plan out what you need from your website. Then you can talk with potential website developers who can assist and work out what option will work with YOUR requirements.

Your website, for a lot of customers, will be their first impression of your business regardless of what product or service you're offering, so take it seriously and plan, plan, plan.

Start with what your website needs to say, look and feel like. Questions to answer:

- What is the purpose of your website? Selling something or providing information.
- Who are you targeting? Refer to your target audiences that you created in the earlier chapter.
- What problem are you solving for customers?
- Will you be offering a product – how many products and variations will you have? This needs to be broken down into

categories, for clothing for example every range, style, colour – all the ways you want to present your product to your customer.

- How will products be ranged in style, sizes, colours, category?
- If it's a service – how many services? Will they need their own page or be grouped together? Think about if you are wanting to sell information that is downloadable and how this needs to be shown across the pages on your site.
- Budget – what is your budget to get your website completed?
- Training – will you need training to assist in the running of the back end of the website?
- What pages do you need to have?
  - Home page.
  - Product/service page(s).
  - Blog page(s).
  - Terms and conditions.
  - Privacy policy.
  - FAQs.
  - About page.
- Will you need your social media pages linked to the website? If so, which ones?
- If you offer a product or service – how are the customers paying? These payment gateways need to be able to be integrated with your website.
- What accounting software are you using? Does this need to have a feed sending invoices every day for your bookkeeping?
- Aesthetics – colours and fonts that match your branding and logo, can that be used on your selected platform?
- Customer experience – will customers be viewing on mobile or desktop?

Then there is the technical stuff, referred to as UX and UI.

UX is the user experience, and that is how the customers experience a product or service. UI is the user interface which refers to the aesthetic elements that people interact with. This area is best left to professionals. Many people build websites to look a certain way – hello, me – but this doesn't mean they will lead to conversions. You need conversions as they are your sales! I learned that whilst I had a lot of information on my website, it did not allow the customers to scroll through easily and it wasn't offering the shoppers the right information about the brand and the offer.

If your conversion rate is too low, it won't matter what marketing you do, as there is a lower chance that people will buy your product or service. Put this at the top of the list when building your website. If you start strong and work all the other things into this, you have a greater chance of getting more sales.

Back end:
- How easily can you update or add items yourself?
- What reporting or analytics will you be able to access?
- How will fulfilment of sold items work?
- How will blogs be added?
- Can marketing be run through the website? How easily can it be created?

Every page is just as important as the others and needs to be thought out. I tend to draw up sketches of each page highlighting exactly the look I want, and I add detail to every page and an overview, so my website developer knows what my desired outcome is. She then works out what the best solution is. Remember, we talked about this earlier, words are great but the more visuals you can show others, the more chance you will have an outcome that is what you are expecting, as there is no room for misinterpretation.

Let's talk the roles of the key pages.

HOME PAGE: THE MOST IMPORTANT PAGE

This is the initial page most of your visitors will land on and it is the very first impression. This is really a summary page that acts as a teaser to appeal to your visitor's interest and hopefully will prompt them to look further into your brand in more pages.

There are some keys things to have on your home page, including an overview of who the brand is and how your offer is different, evidence of claims and calls to action. Sales! You want your customer experience to be that your website is easy to navigate and they can easily make the calls to action (CTA, in short) they want. This could be sending them to view products, specific collections or read blogs about the topic they are interested in.

Your menu is there to guide your customers through your website; it needs to be clearly visible and should be easy to navigate. *The Cut* team recommend looking at your menus as primary and secondary.

Your primary menu is products- and sales-related options. Secondary covers your About Us page, blogs, FAQs etc.

I learned in my business that design is not more important than functionality, and in particular, user experience. We initially built a website that had so much copy and data but didn't encourage CTAs within the home page and meant we did not have a great conversion rate, in turn costing the business many missed opportunities.

PRODUCT OR SERVICE PAGES

The role of this page is very simple: it's about closing the sale. Every product or service you offer needs to have a detailed information and answer questions. Being informative and detailed in your descriptions is positive for both your customer experience and the organic growth you will receive from Google (more about SEO and Google rankings soon). Every product or service needs different wording as repetition will also harm your rankings. Even if two products are similar, describe them differently to enhance the customer experience.

If you have a product, ensure you have great images. Check you have clear images that have been compressed before loading them to the website. Loading images that are too big will slow your website down, hurting your customer's experience and this in turn can harm your domain ratings with Google.

Products need images to allow customers to see the variants or options you have available and showcase all angles of the products, so the shoppers have clear expectations of what they are receiving.

Descriptions should be emotive, but also cover the features and benefits along with any dimensions and all the details that a customer needs. Having all the correct details ensures customers don't need to leave the shopping page and look around your website to find answers, making it as accessible for them as possible.

Detail is great for customers, it will allow them to make a strong decision to hopefully purchase your product/services. If they are unsure, they may leave your site and find another brand that offers clearer descriptions that make them more comfortable to buy. If developing a website with a lot of copy, developers can add coding to minimise the words so customers do not have to read it all but can click to expand if they choose to. If you are running apparel of any sort, include a link to your sizing chart on every product page to enhance the shopper's experience and make it simple for them to check sizing and place an order. Think about it like a fitting room in a retail store, the sales team walk in often to check on customers in the fitting room to see if they need help with sizing. Having a size chart there offers the same option for your customers.

Think about all the information the customer needs so they can make an informed decision. Be transparent in the details so your customers don't get to the checkout and realise there are additional fees you have not covered before, meaning they will abandon the cart.

BLOG PAGES

Blogs are GOLD on your website. They offer your customer information that will benefit them and build the authority of your brand as an industry expert. Plus they can act as great content for email marketing that is sent to your database which will assist with you SEO (search engine optimisation).

This means that the words in your blog work to help build organic Google rankings. This is the way Google recognises websites that answer questions and offer answers to people. The more questions and information your website provides, the more your website can move up the rankings on Google searches organically, which is free advertising for your business.

I was once advised that blogs need to be at least four hundred words to offer the best value to the SEO practice. Whether that is

100% accurate or not, four hundred words is quite small, and I use this as the benchmark for all the blogs I write and load onto the websites.

Coming up with ideas is all about thinking of targeted questions or topics that are relevant to your field of expertise, making sure it all ties into your brand and is relevant. A brand that sells tyres would not add a blog talking about the benefits of bamboo fabric just to add a blog, so look at the alignment and benefit to your target market.

You can write all blogs in a Word document so you can check the word count online. This will allow you to see where you are at as you write and brainstorm. You will be amazed at how quickly the four hundred word count lands on your pages.

As mentioned before, this content can also offer benefits in multiple areas, including marketing an event through your blog, you can add a link or CTA that is a specific offer relatable to the topic at hand, and you can create a video version for your YouTube channel for customers to find and even use this for your social posts or stories to keep customers and clients engaged with the brand, this can then be embedded into the blog on your website and offers another interactions for your customers.

Blogs can create large volumes of traffic for years to come – currently there is one of our blogs that still receives over four thousand views per month around the globe. This doesn't mean these are all potential customers, however, it offers us a great introduction to many people we may not have reached otherwise.

TERMS & CONDITIONS AND PRIVACY POLICY

I have grouped these pages together as they are important legal documents you need to consider for your website. I designed my first draft of these by reviewing about ten other websites first and seeing the keys points I would need to include. I then went and met with my lawyers to finalise these documents. Doing it this way allowed me to save time and money with the lawyers and get this completed quickly and written specifically for my business and customer base.

Too many businesses leave this or do not update the basic policy or terms that some websites come with. Whilst you can use and customise these agreements or use some of the free online resources that are available, I would always recommend running these past a lawyer to ensure that you are protected with your liability. Businesses trading in consumables, body products and children's categories are ones that can have the largest issues if you are not fully aware of the laws, so invest the money in a legal representative for peace of mind from the start.

The terms and conditions are the document that is your contract of sale, for you and your customers. This will also then help form your website FAQs.

FAQs – FREQUENTLY ASKED QUESTIONS

My favourite page on any website. Customers want to know stuff. What are the returns, refund or exchange policy? How long do I have to wait to get my item shipped? Are sale items refundable?

Your FAQs allow customers to get their questions answered twenty-four seven and can reduce the number of questions you have to answer repeatedly, freeing yourself up to work on other things within the business.

The best way I found to start building my FAQs was again by looking at five to ten websites that are similar, checking larger and smaller companies. Review all the FAQs, see what similarities there are as this will help build the initial questions you know you need to answer. Then also review your terms and conditions. Are there any key things a customer will need to know? For example, if you do not offer exchange or credit on sale items, ensure this is included here for ease of viewing. You can either have one list for FAQs or break them into different subheadings – again, this is a decision you should make once you have all your FAQs written out.

The answers need to be clear and match your terms and conditions, everything needs to be aligned and state the same message.

TIP

Include a section on shipping for product-based businesses. We have always had a note regarding the proposed delivery times for items, however, as we use a third party for the shipping, we are not liable for any delays that occur. The past couple of years has shown the importance of having this in place from when we began trading, it meant customers had a clear message and therefore if any issues arose we were able to refer to our policy, terms and conditions and FAQs.

ABOUT PAGE

Having an about page is a great way to showcase the 'why' behind the brand and give greater detail into the brand story. Customers can connect and get a great sense of the brand. If possible, include some images that are relatable to you, the team, or the product/service to help tell the story.

LINKING YOUR SOCIAL MEDIA PAGES

Having the links to all social media pages in the footer or some-where on your website is a great idea and allows for customers to click through easily to view them. Many companies have started adding their Instagram feed to the home page on their websites and it piques the interest of the visitor, giving them a better insight into the brand and offering. It may even increase fol-lowers as customers might not be buying yet, but like the look of the feed and want to follow. This can in turn lead to a future customer for your business.

TIP

Create a vision board for your website. Look at other websites you like – consider the look, feel or functionality to help bring your vision to life.

SEO AND YOUR WEBSITE

SEO is something I had no idea about when we started. I thought that we would just do what looks pretty and nice with some rel-evant words and then we would be set, and as people got onto the website our rankings would grow – wrong!

From my experience, SEO is an integral part of having a successful online business. You want to appear high up in the rankings, it's an area you want to be winning in.

SEO is a long-term game, you don't receive wins overnight

and you need to be prepared for this. On average it will take ninety days before you can see the wins from good SEO work.

You can pay for ads to increase your visibility, but not all businesses have that option due to lack of funding or advertising restrictions. Shisha Works falls into that category, and I must be careful as the products are for people over the age of eighteen and there is no advertising of any sort allowed. Organic searches and social media channels are the only options for visibility, so being focused on SEO is extremely important for the business.

This is an area that experts have needed to be involved in for my business, as I do not have the necessary skills to really make a difference. You may have the knowledge or the time to educate yourself in this area, and power to you if you do, as this will make a big difference when you set up.

If you are like me and don't have this experience, you don't have to spend a fortune, but you need to understand some key elements like: H1 titles, H2 titles, meta tags and keywords and searched questions. Or find professionals that can assist your business with this and help you gain understanding.

There are multiple areas of SEO, and they all offer different things for your business and website.

As you start researching SEO or commence talks with specialists, you will start also hearing about backlinks to help with your domain ranking. These areas are all important and can have a super positive effect on your brand's website, or if not actioned correctly, can have a negative impact that can cost you traffic and sales.

I have had good and bad experiences with my businesses, and I wanted to ensure that I provide you with as much understanding as I can, so that when you go down the 'rabbit hole' you can slide down and start exploring with as much confidence as I can offer.

My SEO summary, from my journey's experience, so you can google each of these areas to do a deep dive to gain further understanding and in-depth knowledge:

KEYWORDS

You need to use keywords across your website pages to help Google understand what your business offers. Keywords need to be useful and not just on the page to be there but offer answers to questions.

CONTENT

Be original; duplicating content across multiple pages can be detrimental to your website. This is on product pages also. Use unique copy that is emotive and informative. Do not copy and paste from others, your content needs to be original.

H1, H2 AND META DESCRIPTIONS

These are how Google finds your pages. These need to be a certain length in characters and are on EVERY page across your website. Make them count. Many businesses will fill all these headers and tags under the website or site health checks. Ensure that this is completed very early on as they are simple fixes that should be part of the low-hanging fruit actions to be completed quickly.

404 ERROR MESSAGES

These errors are again part of the basic site health tests that should be run. These errors can easily damage rankings and authority for your site. A 404 error is when Google cannot direct the traffic to the page as it is not found. You can fix this by either republishing the page that is removed in error, or your web developer will redirect the traffic to an alternate page.

IMAGES

Clear images that are correctly named with your brand name referenced. Ensure images are compressed to ensure they do not increase website loading times as this can decrease your user experience and damage your domain authority.

DR – DOMAIN AUTHORITY

This is a number that Google uses to rank your business, and this can increase and decrease for multiple reasons. All the above topics aid in this ranking along with your backlinks.

BACKLINKS

These again can be gold for your business and rankings if completed correctly, but if wrongly completed they can be very harmful.

A backlink is a link via another website, normally through an article that shows credibility to your business or brand. Every link has a domain ranking between 1–100. The higher the domain ranking, the better your website. My understanding is that best practice is to try for DRs over thirty. The backlinks with DRs of less than twenty are normally the easier ones to obtain but offer very little authority to your website and your ranking but will probably be free and easier to obtain.

Regardless of the ranking, a BIG BIG BIG lesson I have

recently learned is about backlinks being broken into two sub-categories: either NOFOLLOW or DOFOLLOW. You want to ensure that all the backlinks your business gets are DOFOLLOW. The NOFOLLOW ones are no benefit to your business.

The great news is everything in SEO is actually reportable. SEO specialists all have access to different online systems to check data and provide insights.

Backlinks are no different; there is a report that can be found called AHREFS. This report helped me find specific issues and discrepancies. This report shows what DR ranking and quantity your business has. Just like errors with headers/titles and meta tags on website pages. This is all reportable, so when in doubt ask for the reports.

The reason I wanted to share these learnings is that when you decide to hire a SEO specialist to work with your brand, you may find that you enter a contract for six to twelve months for a set monthly fee, and I want to ensure you can negotiate the contract with specific terms.

As I have been in the position with a larger company who offered my business the world, but in fact our business started going backwards with our traffic and conversion from month five of our contract, I had to level up my knowledge to ensure that the business would not continue to suffer. The sad part is that as many of us are not educated in this specific area, we can end up being more trusting of the 'professionals' and this is not always the best path to take. The cost to my business financially was extreme and so was the time wasted chasing the account manager to take actions to help stop the damage they had caused.

I wish I had the knowledge I have today back then, so I wouldn't have wasted my time and I would have altered my contract even further with the business prior to signing.

My key questions prior to signing with an SEO specialist:

1. What is included in site health checks?
2. Will all headers, tags and error messages be fixed 100% once the site health check is completed?
3. How many keywords will be targeted every month? Twenty, thirty, fify plus? Be specific.
4. What is the minimum DR ranking on backlinks they will be providing? Example, twenty or higher?
5. What guarantee does the company offer around the DR rankings and DOFOLLOW and NOFOLLOW backlinks?
6. What reporting will they be offering? I would not accept anything less than one report per month with all the actions completed and updated information. You need to stay on top of this and have the opportunity to discuss how this is working for your business.
7. What are the campaign goals?
8. How are they measurable? Get the specifics.
9. What happens if targets or goals are not met?

Google Search Consoles, Google Analytics and My Business Google accounts all fall under SEO work. You will also need to have these set up to help with analytics to ensure that the best reporting is available for yourself or whoever is covering this for you.

I am not even going to try and go into details on all the Google applications mentioned above because I am not knowledgeable, but I am sure as you head down this path you will learn more about each area and the benefit to your brand, or will find an individual or business who can help you do this.

Finding the specialist that suits your business is about where you see the benefit and bang for your buck. Just because someone is a smaller business or the largest in town, does not make them any more qualified to work with your brand.

In summary, there are many different SEO areas for your business: on-page SEO, off-page SEO, image SEO and content strategy, just to name a few. Which ones are you going to investigate for your business?

TIP 1

Please ensure you talk at length with each business you are looking at working with and spend the time getting to know someone, not just via emails. Ask questions, and I recommend thinking about how you get along personality-wise. I always treat every new potential contact like an interview process. This gives both parties the opportunity to see if your personalities gel well together. Is the communication easy? Follow up with everything you discuss in writing to cover both parties and ensure that expectations are outlined clearly.

TIP 2

Ask for examples of previous work they have done in your field so you can see how they understand your category. Most businesses will happily supply some references to assist. In the event they cannot, you need to decide if this is the right path for your business.

TIP 3

SEO work can be time-consuming – by that I mean it takes time to start working. If you are looking at signing up with a company to do this work for you, see if you can negotiate a shorter-term contract so you are not stuck in anything long-term, in case this does not work out as per the example I provided above.

TIP 4

Ensure the work is all on a contract so you can make sure that there are key deliverables for the project length so the work can be measured. Please refer back to the list of questions I have provided.

TIP 5

Spending money on advertising is not always the answer for increasing sales; sometimes, completing more work on your website, SEO and blogging can be more beneficial to your business and can be executed for smaller fees than an advertising campaign.

SHOPIFY THEMES

With Shopify you can select from free or paid themes, and now Shopify 2.0 has been released, adding even more options for you. The themes are there to act as a template and offer you the option to customise it slightly to represent your brand online.

When you set up your website plan and note everything you need from a website, if you head down the Shopify path this will also then allow you to find the theme that is best suited.

The reason you do this is to minimise the apps and coding needed to get your business up and running. There are thousands of themes available and you can change them when you wish. Also you will need the help of a developer, but it is simple to upgrade as your business is growing and evolving.

I chose to update our themes about three years into one of my businesses and twelve months into the other. Why? The business needs had changed, and I needed a theme that offered more. This change allowed me to decrease the apps or plug-ins we were using, in turn reducing the costs for the monthly running.

APPS

Apps are available to help build out your website. I have been told to minimise the number of apps you use as they can slow the website speed, and this, as mentioned earlier, can damage your DR. You want to maximise this as much as you can.

With ELC we must use a special app for the images to be different for every size of garment on the online store. This app does slow the speed of our website as it requires more images to be uploaded, however, the benefit to our business outweighs the slow speed.

Apps can be free, but most are charged for use each month. When looking at apps, note that most app costs quoted are monthly charges in USD. Read reviews and look at the examples developers have provided. There are many forums across the web where you can connect with other people to assist with information and decisions on apps.

TIP

Read all the fine print and understand what the app needs access to in your website prior to joining.

VISUALS

Looking at the branding, I knew I wanted to have some visual elements representing the brand website, however, this was not as easy as I thought. I found that the visuals I wanted to have, including background patterns like wallpaper, would not be able to be included, or if I did add them my site speed would drop dramatically. This is why planning is key when deciding which platform will suit your needs best. Every platform is different, but the good news is they are all set up to assist the best outcome and you just need to work with specialists who can direct you once you provide them with your plan and requirements.

POP-UP AND NEWSLETTER SIGN UP

There are many websites that flood you with pop-ups the minute you enter, for me personally this drives me nuts, especially if you cannot see how to exit out of them. It is a proven marketing method that you can create an offer to entice your customers to sign up, think about this, however, it can have a negative impact on your DR if you have too many.

What will your customers be expecting? How will it work for them? If you are doing pop-ups, what will your offer be? Plan this carefully and think about what your customer will benefit from, not what you do and don't like.

Think about clever ways to get your customers signing up to your mailing list or newsletter; your database is one of your greatest assets, it costs a business a lot less to target a warm lead than a cold lead, and if they have already shown interest in your brand, then half the work has been done. Look after them.

We started with Mailchimp but migrated across to Shopify

Marketing when this feature became available, and we decreased our spend and increased our frequency of electronic direct mail (EDM) to our customers, in turn creating more profitable sales events.

There are a number of marketing tools and programs available to use in conjunction with your website like Mailchimp, Klaviyo, Moosend, HubSpot, Sendinblue and the list goes on. Think about this carefully from the start as your database and customer communication is one of the most important areas of your business.

I had the pleasure of working with Ben and the team from *The Cut,* who are Shopify experts, on our website update, and they offered some great tips for people when thinking about their websites:

1. Find the niche that fits you and your focus and passion.
2. Develop your brand for your customer, not yourself.
3. Keep it simple, strong and legible.
4. Show what life is like with your products in it.
5. Make your brand something to reach for.
6. Speak to your customers like it's a two-way conversation, because it is.
7. Customer engagement comes first, then conversion.
8. Images:
   - Look beautiful.
   - Are high quality.
   - Show benefits.
9. Statement:
   - Showcase key benefit(s).
   - How you help customers.
   - What makes you awesome.

10. Expand:
- – Expand on your offering.
- – Show more of your story.
- – Increase engagement with your customer.

In closing, always think about mobile presentation and this will most likely be the primary device your customers use when viewing your website.

ACTIONS

- Create website planner – including written copy and imagery.
- Build your plan for SEO strategy.
- Build plan for website imagery.
- Research marketing software for your business.
- Review your plan – is it clear, structured well for customers' journeys to be smooth and simple and allow them to purchase easily?

SELF-CHECK-IN TIME

Wow, that was a big chapter with a lot of information, how are you feeling?

Building websites can be a big process, so ensure you break it down and work through it strategically. If you are feeling like it is too much, reach out for some help from networking groups like: Like Minded Bitches Drinking Wine, Business Chicks or another in your local area – and you can always take a break and come back to it.

If you are super excited about this process, start your research and planning, build it with as much detail as possible to get yourself ready to chat with developers with a clear plan.

Some great books to help get you motivated if you want to keep inspired are:

- Tony Robbins – *Awaken the Giant Within.*
- Gabrielle Berstein – *The Universe Has Your Back.*
- Rhonda Byrne – *The Secret.*

When I have a moment I seem to come back to one of these three audiobooks or another title from these incredible authors, they always seem to help get me back into the positive mindset.

NOTES

CHAPTER 11

SOCIAL MEDIA

'With social media it should be quality over quantity.'
– Danielle Sady

Social media can become one of the most overwhelming areas in running a startup business, especially if you are like me and struggle to build content for all the different areas and find yourself getting overwhelmed and frustrated trying to keep up with the latest algorithm or trends emerging online.

There are so many platforms to choose from, and you need to know you do not need to be on them all. When starting out you need to think about the platforms that will be aligned with your audience and brand.

Breaking it down this way will help remove some of the pressure within your businesses' social media expectations. In turn this will then make you more visible to your target market and give you the opportunity to interact regularly with your audience.

The biggest key with any platform is to ensure that you post relevant content that is useful to the audience you are targeting. I personally have gained understanding on most social media platforms via online forums and paid courses so I could start adding value to the platforms we use regularly.

At Everyday Lingerie Co we only utilise Instagram, Facebook, Pinterest, YouTube and LinkedIn to communicate with our audience as these are platforms that we can manage well and add value for our community. Learning early on that quality always wins over quantity was a great lesson. This allowed me to work with the marketing teams to focus on utilising the platforms to the best of their ability, not trying to make it harder than it needed to be and ending up being stressed about what to post.

I am a firm believer in also growing my accounts organically. Meaning that I do not pay for followers or subscribers to give the perception of something. I often struggle when reviewing others' feeds and notice small engagement numbers for content when they have a large following. I would rather grow and have genuine people there celebrating the brand and content, allowing me to have real data about what is appealing to my audience, than trying to distinguish between what's real and what's fake.

The choice will always be yours, but I would always suggest that you think about what it will actually bring to you, and next time you are on a platform, in particular Instagram, if you are looking at a profile with 100,000 followers and wondering how they did it, have a look at the engagement on their posts, is it real or just some 'social media reality'?

Let's look at each platform that you can potentially use within your business in some more detail. This is from what I have learned from my day to day; remember, I do not declare to be a social media expert, but rather have gained my knowledge from my business and engaging with experts and further education and research online.

INSTAGRAM

With over a billion users in 2021 and around 500 million daily users, Instagram is an area to investigate if your target market is included in that demographic.

On this platform it's all about utilising the options as much as you can. You can do posts, Stories, IGTV and Reels. They all have their own place within the app.

To start with, set up your profile well. Once you have your handle – i.e. @everydaylingerieco – then fill in all the details and include in the bio as much as you can whilst fitting into the character limit. Do not just repeat your business name here. Your brand's bio should include words that will help your business appear in searches that your target market will be looking at, what you offer in summary and key points that will benefit your followers who land on your page.

Posts are the images that are on your grid, and you must have an image on every post. The role of the copy that you post with the image is about drawing people in and will hopefully get interaction from your followers.

Start with a grabbing headline or question to give the audience an idea of what you will be discussing, then the body of the copy will give details and end with a question to again promote interaction.

Once your image and copy are in, now you need to look at hashtags. There has always been a lot of debate on where it is best to put the hashtags, either at the end of the post, which some say makes your post more discoverable for people searching on Instagram, and others say to put it in the comments section. You decide, maybe try both options and see which works best for you.

There is a maximum of thirty hashtags per post. If you add all thirty hashtags, please note that it then means that no followers can add a hashtag in the comments section if they want to as you will exceed the maximum allowed.

My plan with hashtags is to break them into categories. I have a list for each business that contains around one hundred to two hundred relevant hashtags. I have them broken into different groups, so I mix up every post with different hashtags to target different accounts. If you use the same ones for every post, you are limiting the reach. I consider the hashtags in three areas: marketing relevance, location and key phrases that people would use to reference the product or service, and my aim is to run with around fifteen to twenty hashtags per post.

The general guide, as I understand it, is that the important interactions on Instagram are in this order, from highest to lowest: save, share, comment, like. This means the more your posts get saved or shared, the more value the platform sees in your page and will then in turn promote this more.

If someone comments on your post, comment back! Interact with your followers and use words not just emojis. I was once told to use a minimum of four-word responses, but I do not know if that is factual or not, I just ensure all my engagements add value and are positive back to my community.

If you get a negative comment, do not allow that to wreck your day or set you back. Use the time to engage and hopefully work through any issue that has been raised.

When we converted across to Australian manufacturing, we had some comments around the pricing. I spent the time engaging with these customers taking them through our manufacturing process, how we use premium-quality materials all custom-made in Australia and that then we also make each garment locally which increases the price, and this was so we could offer customers the highest quality garments. 80% of these customers went on to purchase from our product range and one of them is now one of our largest-spending customers who owns around twenty pairs of ELC underwear and emailed thanking us for explaining and how grateful she was we took the time to explain everything and was so happy she will never wear any other underwear ever again.

My experience has shown that you should post (this is different to your Stories) a maximum of one post in a twenty-four-hour period as it can decrease your interactions if you post more. Once you commence posting, you will start getting the insights from your account and will find out when your audience is engaging best and be able to target times that suit them.

Initially try different times like morning, noon and evening and see how they all fare, then decide the targeted times for your account.

Stories are for more the day-to-day in the business; you can use up to ten hashtags in stories which will need to be added in text or you can add one hashtag via the stickers available. Run polls, ask questions and try different things to get your reach up.

Reels are a short-form video that are like TikTok videos, and they are different from IGTV where you can post up to sixty-minute videos. Reels are really the go-to on this platform now and are definitely something to consider. If you use hashtags on Reels, like all the other content, you have the chance to show up in the top section of hashtags you choose to use.

Reels can be added to your static feed or just in your Reels menu – you choose where this will be shared once you post it. It can be added to your feed and then removed later and left just to be discovered in the Reels feed, the choice is yours.

IGTV is for videos you want to produce and share. With all my IGTVs, I load them to both Instagram and our YouTube channel. These videos are normally ten to sixty minutes in length. Hashtags again need to be used when posting and you can decide if you want the videos to be loaded to your feed or you can hide from the feed and leave it only visible on the IGTV tab of your page.

You also have your Instagram shop that is available for showcasing the products that your business is selling. The shop can be connected via many ecommerce platforms so as you add products to your range, they will be updated to your Instagram shop once you initially connect. There are some limitations, as we learned, with showing the full underwear range for Everyday Lingerie Co, so you may need to review the guidelines before, and you do not need a Facebook shop to connect this feature, but you will need a Facebook page either personal or business.

SUMMARY

- Posts build community, engagement and education on your brand. Aim for saves, shares, likes and follows.
- Stories – behind the scenes, more organic if you wish, adds

value, keeps you top of mind, can build trust and your audience.

- Reels offer opportunity to increase traffic, educate through video and carousels of images.
- IGTV – brand trust, personal connection and help with sales and education of brand.

TIP

- Don't repeat your name in your profile bio, use this line to describe what you do as it's searchable.
- Remove watermarks from other platforms like TikTok before posting on Instagram as they don't like this because it advertises another competing brand.
- Add the tags behind your Story, hiding them, so your Stories look cleaner.
- Use as many of the stickers, questions, GIFs and/or music you can on Stories as the app likes you using the features it has available.
- There are options to add autogenerated captions to videos which is a great idea as many people scroll social media with sound off and including captions can be very beneficial for followers who are hearing impaired to ensure they too can enjoy your content and interact.

FACEBOOK

With 1.79 billion users visiting Facebook daily in 2021, it is said that this is the third most visited website in the world. When posting to Facebook there is no need for hashtags, and you can post without any photos, images or videos, unlike Instagram.

The choice is yours.

Facebook now has Stories just like Instagram and you can post the Stories to both platforms when you load to Instagram, or you can create separate ones for each platform.

We have seen from our experience that you do not need to post as detailed copy as you do with Instagram, but we have always posted the same copy on both platforms to ensure our community receives the same level of detail regardless of the platform they are using.

This is really a platform for those wanting to share longer content with around sixty thousand characters allowed in a regular post.

Like with Instagram, you have the option of running a Facebook shop which offers a catalogue of products for sale from your website for people to view. With Shopify this is all set up via the back end and very seamless.

PINTEREST *(Source of stats – Sprout social and Google)*

If you are selling a product, I was blown away by learning that there are approximately 454 million monthly active users of Pinterest, with 60% being women, and it is reported that between 80–90% of users purchased something based on Pins they saw from brands. So for Everyday Lingerie Co we felt it was a necessary platform we needed to use.

I have created boards when I have been researching personally and saw the benefits of finding specific items and brands through this. The agency we work with manages the account on our behalf, utilising the marketing images we have in our portfolio to showcase the brand, and with the regular work they have been doing, our numbers have been consistently growing and we can see the traffic that this platform is providing for our website.

This is an image-based platform, so you really need to ensure every photo speaks volumes about your brand's product.

TWITTER *(Source of stats – blog.hootsuite.com)*

Reports are currently saying that Twitter has approximately 187 million active users daily and around one billion tweets by users per week, with close to 30% of users being twenty-five to thirty-four years old. Most content can contain up to 280 characters, so much shorter than some others.

This platform is targeted more like headlines and biggest news. According to some reports, images are better content than videos, however, the reports are suggesting that text performs better than images and quotes do better than questions. Overall clear statements with messages that are current work best.

You use hashtags on this platform as per Instagram and TikTok.

TIKTOK

Available in over 150 countries with over one billion users reportedly using the app every month, TikTok was designed for creating and sharing short videos.

You create your account as per the other platforms and then commence recording and loading. All the videos can be created within the app, then you can edit and add your copy or text boxes along with hashtags.

It's suggested you use a maximum of five hashtags that are strategic and related to each video.

With TikTok, it's about more than just short videos; there are different trending music clips, voice overs and singing or dancing trends that can be adapted to your brand in this app.

The point of this is to encourage people to join the trend and create their own versions or adapt them to your business in a fun and enjoyable way, then in return the algorithm rewards this and the videos are more likely to receive views because they are pushed to others who enjoy that trend.

To find out what is currently trending, head to the discovery tab in the app or follow the hashtag #trendalert to find out.

You will receive likes and comments on these posts just like Facebook and Instagram, and the more engagement your profile receives, the more your videos will be pushed to potentially increase viewing.

TIP

When creating videos in TikTok and sharing to your Instagram platform, it's been suggested that you remove the TikTok watermark as most social platforms do not really like promoting others. This can be done through certain apps.

YOUTUBE *(Source of Stats – global media insights.com)*

There are reportedly more than 2.6 billion active users and it's been shared that more than a quarter of the world's population use YouTube every month. Every minute, around five hundred hours of new content is uploaded to the platform.

With eighteen- to twenty-five-year-olds being the largest age group visiting the site every month and over 50% of the audience being people aged eighteen to fifty-six, there is a vast range of potential customers visiting this platform.

The aim of YouTube, since 2005 when it launched, is a video sharing platform that brings a large range of videos all to one place including news, products reviews, music clips, how-to videos and much more.

Your video content here can be the same as what you have created for other platforms, but when loading you need to ensure that you fill in all the relevant fields to get the exposure.

Once you set up your account you upload your video with a title. This can be up to one hundred characters and the focus needs to be on the first thirty words that the customers would focus or search for. Think SEO-style writing when loading to YouTube.

Then create a description for the video with Google in mind again. Use words from the video, answer questions and offer direct links for customers. If this is a blog-style video, the transcript can be added, but remember you can only have up to five thousand characters.

From here you can work through creating all the relevant tags and lists for your videos to be loaded. There are actually many videos regarding how to load to YouTube on Google and YouTube itself to walk you through the entire process.

I recently spoke with a YouTube optimisation specialist who explained to me that having and running a YouTube channel well can really benefit your Google rankings as they are owned by the same company. The video content will lift authority and get the caption SEO optimised which is extremely beneficial. This is something I have not yet been able to deep dive into but a great starting point if you are going to have a lot of video content in your business and/or brand.

LINKEDIN

This is the most professional platform focused on business and networking.

You can set up either a personal page to represent yourself if you are offering a service and/or a business page to showcase what your brand offers.

LinkedIn is like an electronic business card. You can load text only or videos and images with copy. Hashtags are also used on this platform. If you are offering a service, this is a great platform to showcase your career history and summarise what your skill set is.

With brand pages we generally post our blogs to our feed to offer another way to connect with people who are in the industry or with potential customers. Our blogs are focused on education and industry information, and posting one to two times per month has seen our followers consistently grow and engage.

TROLLING

There could be a time when one or more of your accounts is hit by a troll, and you must decide how you wish to handle this. For me, trolling is not tolerated, and our policy is that if anyone trolls our account with a negative or derogatory comment regarding anyone in our marketing, they will be blocked from the page and all comments removed immediately. If they wish to discuss the brand, we will engage, but comments about people in our advertising or marketing material will never be tolerated, so decide this early on to ensure that you have a plan and can action this if it happens.

Don't allow negative comments to discourage you from what you are building, sometimes people just have the need to say inappropriate things that can be hurtful, but they are easily said behind a keyboard. Rise above it and have a plan so you know how to deal with this if it unfortunately does happen, but remember you can find ways to not let this beat you down or discourage you.

CREATING THE CONTENT

Canva is the platform I use, and as mentioned earlier, there are so many features to assist you in creating great content that is on brand and allows you to look like you have a professional design team behind you even when you do not.

For a small yearly fee, you can use many different platforms that can save you the money of working with a designer whilst you get your business up and running. If you take the time to play around and learn the platform you select, you can be a creative pro that creates content every month on brand and looks so professional for a tenth of the price you would pay a company each month.

Alternatively, there are amazing social media companies that are operating around the globe that can really help, either through their online education programs in social media training, or on a contract basis that they run your entire social media accounts each month for a fee.

If your cashflow permits and you feel this area is overwhelming, start investigating social media creators or businesses that may align with your brand and can work in with your budget to help you get started.

CONTENT PLANNING

All my content, including posts, Stories, videos and LinkedIn updates are scheduled in a planner by month. I work a month ahead at a time so I can see how everything I am posting ties together and showcases a variety of content to my audience.

Too many businesses post product, product and product. I can say this with conviction as I know that Shisha Works was one of those companies at the beginning. I could not understand why there was no gaining of potential customers from posts. I then completed an online course, and some individuals were talking about the audience and the value your social pages offered them. The light bulb went on – the business was not offering value, it was just showing the audience the website catalogue day in day out every month. Then we created categorised themes for each business which broke posts up and showcased keys areas: product, education, inspiration and behind the scenes, which we built the monthly planners around and offered benefit to the followers.

This allows your customers to learn facts that are industry related, see what's new, get educated on different product benefits and features rather than sales and finally get to know the face or team behind your brand.

The changes increased engagement, and it was obvious the community wanted to learn more about the who, why and how the brand came to life. There are still posts in the mix that are sales and about product, but it's now more about information, and the sales and quick notes are more for Stories.

CONTENT SCHEDULING

You have so much to do when starting out that remembering to post content can easily slip your mind. As you have already mapped out your week, two weeks or month in advance, you can use one of the many scheduling systems that are around to assist. Over the years I have used Buffer with both the free option and paid service, Canva planner schedule tool and Greatly Social for a client that only runs an Instagram account.

When looking into all the scheduling tools available, remember to check what each plan offers and how many posts can be scheduled, this is particularly relevant when you are using free account options. Do you need Facebook Business Manager? If so, you will need a Facebook account that has authority over the other social media pages. You do not have to go down this path, you can just run Instagram on its own also, but look for the program that will offer exactly what you need.

TIP

Post content that adds value. Quality over quantity is the key. If you are posting just to fill the space, you are posting for the wrong reason. You have limited time to make your impression – make it count.

Finally, setting up a Linktree account can be a great addition to your Instagram bio. Linktree is a service that allows you to offer links to key pages or websites for your business. The account can be set up for free and themed. You then add links to your website, blogs, LinkedIn, YouTube or wherever you wish to offer customers easy access. It's a great tool for businesses that take bookings through online services, you can add a button for customers or clients to connect directly to your booking system seamlessly and easily without leaving your page.

Then add the link for your Linktree account to your social media profile for your followers by coping the link from the account set-up page, add to Instagram in the website area in the bio section.

ACTIONS

- Develop your business plan for what platforms you will be working with.
  - How often will you be posting on each platform (create a flow chart to see the workload)?
- Develop your social media planner template that allows you to build your plan.
  - Build by platform.
  - Note times for posting, dates, copy and hashtags.
- If able, investigate possible businesses if you wish to outsource social media.
- Research platforms such as Canva for options to professionally build your marketing/social media items.
- Look into setting up your Linktree account and add to your social media profile for your followers.

SELF-CHECK-IN TIME

How are you feeling?

Talk to other small business owners to understand how they are working their social media plans into their business; you may find some great tips and tricks they have learned, or book a meeting with a social media agency or consultant to gain more insight.

As always, if you are feeling like this is a lot, take some time out. When you are ready, come back and break down your plans or chat with someone in your support network to help create your action plans.

If you don't find any of the above suggestions work, go back to just having some you time; if you can go and do something that you are passionate about and take time off from planning to refresh, and when you are ready you can begin again.

NOTES

CHAPTER 12

INFLUENCERS, BRAND AMBASSADORS AND COLLABORATIONS

'The largest followers do not equal the greatest returns when collaborating on social media.' – Danielle Sady

Thanks to people like Kim Kardashian changing the way we use Instagram, an entire world of advertising opportunities has opened for businesses with influencers, brand ambassadors and collaborations.

INFLUENCERS

Influencers are classed in different groups that depend on their total number of followers. Many people have different names, but below shows a chart of one of the ways influencer levels can be described or categorised.

Influencer Type	Follower Range
Nano	1,000 to 10,000
Micro	10,000 to 50,000
Mid	50,000 to 500,000
Macro	500,000 to 1 million
Celebrity or Mega	1 million plus

The role of an influencer is to build an audience based on being an 'expert' and show knowledge on a specific topic or area. Influencers can assist with sharing your brand story and product or service, but you need to select the ones that share your target market if you want to collaborate or work with them as brand ambassadors.

Before you even start looking for potential influencers or brand ambassadors, you need to know what you want to achieve from this.

START BY BUILDING YOUR PLAN OR GUIDE

How many influencers do you want to work with a month?

Do you have a budget for this, if so, what is the budget per month? This is for paid influencers and the stock or service you will be investing.

What product or service will you be offering? Detail exactly what will be shipped if you are product based.

What will be expected in return? Be specific, how many posts, Stories, Reels etc.

When starting out you may find that you do not have a budget that can be spent on influencers, and that works also, but you need to be aware of what you are offering and the return that both parties will receive.

If you hand-make your range or run with small stock holdings, be thoughtful with your plan. Having five items in stock and sending these to four influencers may be counterproductive as you will only have one piece remaining and people hopefully will want to purchase this item. If they come to shop and the item is sold out, you have cost yourself the sale.

Once your planning is complete it is time to start looking at who you want to work with.

What's the best way to create a list of potential brand ambassadors and influencers?

Start by following potential influencers; my advice is to be genuinely interested in the person you are going to work with. Selecting someone based solely on their followers won't always end well.

Look for accounts where you can see that the target market is similar, that they showcase the same values as your brand, that the look and feel of the feed aligns with your brands.

Once you have a starting list, add and remove to this list as you work through initial emails or contact with the influencers, in general this should be a working document, not a set and forget. It will build over time and allow you to have a solid list of what is happening in this area of your business and act as a reminder for follow-ups.

Next, once you have found your top three, five or ten, look at their engagement, the amount that can work within your budget and stock restraints.

How many likes and comments are they getting on posts?

Are the comments and likes coming from the desired audience? Spend the time reviewing this. If you are a female-targeted product and all the comments are from men, this may not be the influencer for you or your brand.

Do some calculations to see if their engagement is low, average or high.

Instagram influencer or account engagement calculations:

Engagement = (likes + comments) / followers x 100.

Engagement = (likes + comments + saves) / impressions x 100.

Between 1–3.5% is an average engagement and over 3.5% is considered high engagement.

TIP

Log into Instagram on your desktop as it can be easier to see the actual likes and comments of a potential influencer, then select the last ten or twelve posts. Add together the total likes and comments, then divide by the total number of posts you are viewing (ten or twelve) then use that number to divide by total followers x 100. This will give you a rough idea of potential engagement prior to reaching out.

Once you have your shortlist, start reaching out either via direct message or the contact details such as email if they are listed on their profile.

HOW TO REACH OUT TO POTENTIAL INFLUENCERS FOR A COLLABORATION

Make sure each outreach is personal, professional, offers insight to the brand and the reason for reaching out. Include why you believe they would be a good fit and some key information around the campaign you would like to run if they are interested. Some influencers can get hundreds of messages, so you want to stand out from the crowd. Sending the same message copy and pasted across to a group of influencers won't get a high return, it will also seem as if you are not genuinely interested in the collaboration with them. It won't be received very well.

Include your contact details so they can get back to you via message, email or call.

A great trick I have used numerous times is to send a personalised video message; this has worked well for me as people can get to know the face behind the brand and really see that this is for them, not a copy and paste message that a hundred others will also be receiving.

After one week, if you have not heard back, you can choose to send another message or email politely saying why you are following up. Try to understand that they could have a full book currently or your brand may not be right for them. It is not personal if you don't hear back – remember, this is a business.

On the flip side, if you do you hear back, that's amazing. Now you need to discuss engagement and the rates applicable as I have learned firsthand that some influencers do purchase followers.

You also now can ask for some live statistics, a simple photo of this is easy for them to send across or from their media kit, just to be sure.

Most influencers will be happy to provide this as they are proud of what they are achieving. Once you are satisfied and all preliminary talks have been completed and you both wish to proceed, now you need to formalise the agreement regardless of a paid or product contract deal. It's always best to have an agreement or contract in place.

Contracts or agreements need to include:

- Your business name and full contact details.
- Influencer's details:
  - Full name.
  - Contact email.
  - Contact phone number.
  - Postal address, at a minimum, for goods to be shipped to.
  - Terms of the agreement.
  - Number of posts, Stories (is it one or two slides) and/or Reels to be delivered in detail, including quantities.
  - Due date for actions, example: three weeks from receiving of stock.
  - Payment or total stock value to be received for this work.
- List the business hashtags that must be included in postings.
- Any special conditions you have agreed on. If this is a brand ambassador deal you would include the length of term. Is the influencer agreeing to work exclusively with your brand and will not work with other brands that are seen as rivals or competitors? If so, there is a time limit on that. Please note if you are running collaborations in exchange for goods and not payment, please don't ask for this from an influencer. They in most cases would never post similar brands in a short period of time, but discuss this so everyone is clear.
- Are you able to reshare images? If so, in what forum, on socials only or can the images they provide be used for all your marketing and what is the expiry on the use, if any?
- The date and signatures from both parties.

This is the best way to protect both parties and ensure that the terms and conditions are met by both you and the influencer or brand ambassador you are working on this collaboration with.

As with all contracts or agreements you use within your business, there are plenty of amazing online resources, but we always do recommend that, regardless of if you write them yourself or use an online resource, you have a legal representative check over the agreement to ensure that all parties are covered.

COLLABORATING WITH OTHER BUSINESSES

You can also look to other businesses for collaborations, it doesn't have to be a singular person. There are many brands that support each other to showcase the benefits of their brands. Think about the alignment and how it will serve your customers. How do the products work together? Chat with other potential business owners. Do they love your products and brand and do you feel the same about theirs? Even if this is a one-off collaboration, you can learn from each other and they may even have some recommendations of influencers that worked for their business. One of the biggest influencers I worked with was a recommendation from another business, and I am so glad I took the advice, we both had fashion businesses that catered for a large size selection, and we were able to get sales in four countries after one post from this incredible influencer.

Don't get stung by thinking that a large number of followers guarantees returns.

When starting out we all want to start with hundreds of orders every day, and this can happen, but it's the exception to the rule. A new brand takes time to build.

Looking for influencers with the largest following is normally going to come with a price, and it's a big one. For example, it was reported in 2021 that it costs around $400,000 to $1 million for one post by Kylie Jenner, Ariana Grande, Selena Gomez or Kim Kardashian. If you have the money and feel this is the best ad spend and potential return on investment, go for it, but many startup businesses have worked with nano and micro influencers to build their profile and have been successful as they have genuine engagement happening. What I mean by that is, think about how many celebrity profiles you follow, how much do you engage with their feed? Have you ever purchased anything they have advertised?

BRAND AMBASSADORS

The difference between a one-off post agreement and a brand ambassador is that with an ambassador you will normally have an agreement for a set length of time, for example three or six months. For this type of agreement you need to ensure that all parties stick to the due dates. Include a clause that highlights that if the terms are not met what the consequences will be. Will the contract be terminated or will they be expected to pay retail for the goods?

I also suggest that the ambassadors are offered an incentive if they want to purchase additional items from your business. It can be a percentage or dollar amount discount – you decide what your business can afford and what will benefit the mutual agreement.

In conclusion, I have personally had good and bad experiences with all the above and since implementing the written agreements I have found that 95–99% of agreements are completed without any issues, however, there is always some risk. I start every agreement with the details and highlight clearly that I want the influencer to try our products obligation free first. We will sign the agreement and post the stock, if for any reason the influencer doesn't like or finds the products don't work for them, they can return all the garments obligation free if they advise us within seven days of receiving the parcel. We email across a return shipping label and then the agreement ends. This may not work for you but should be considered when starting out so you can get your foot in the door and start building your brand's reputation.

As with most areas of the business, I run an Excel spreadsheet with all the influencers' details along with agreement terms so I can manage and review to ensure all the dates and deadlines are met; this minimises confusion or the chance to forget. Have something set up with your outline by month, this will allow you to see when you need to run searches or find contacts to work with that will tie in with new product launches, key dates or just when the retail sector slows and allow you to push for brand presence and hype. It's time to think about how you want this area to work for you within your business.

TIP
Have written agreements that contain all details to protect both parties so there is no room for misunderstanding.

ACTIONS
- Create an influencer/collaboration agreement template (ensure you have a legal representative review).
- Create your business budget for collaborations, break this

down by month.

- Research potential influencers that align with your brand.
- Create a shortlist of influencers.
- Start outreach when the time suits.

SELF-CHECK-IN TIME

How are you feeling?

Are you excited to start chatting with potential influencers or does it feel daunting?

If you are excited, start building your list and begin checking to see how this could work.

If you are feeling overwhelmed, take some time to step away from this work for now and go and have some time for yourself. Remember to think about how far you have come and celebrate that, even if this or one of the other chapters is feeling hard. Everyone has their expertise, and look at the opportunities where you can learn and grow.

If you need extra help, reach out to your network and ask for assistance.

NOTES

CHAPTER 13

MINDSET

*'It's what you practise in private that you will be
rewarded for in public.' – Tony Robbins*

Throughout your entire journey you need to be physically and
mentally ready to complete this marathon. I say physically and
mentally because both areas come into play.

It is easy sometimes, particularly when starting out, to look
at others and see the financial success they have because of their
business and start comparing yourself to others, but this is not
helpful or productive for you. Every business was once a startup
and every owner has walked in your shoes at one point. They too
have experienced the challenges and have worked through them,
that is why they are standing where they are now, and you can too.

Social media, for some, will be a catalyst for self-doubt, others
will find it empowering or motivating. I know, for me, it was all
of the above. At times I thought I needed to change to be in line
with what I saw others doing, and the truth was, I didn't. That

is their journey, not mine. It took me some time to really understand and believe this. We all have doubts. We all hit hurdles or challenges along the way, but how you manage these when they arise is the key.

Physically you need to be healthy. This means having good sleep routines to allow your mind and body to rest. As business owners we tend to think we need to work around the clock and push ourselves to exhaustion to be successful. The reality is some days the hours will be long; however, this is not how every day should be. Every waking moment working to keep your business running won't make you any more successful – if anything, you will probably make more mistakes and feel like throwing in the towel as fatigue is very real.

Studies show lack of sleep can lead to slowed thinking, mood shifts, low energy levels, decreased memory, along with potential health issues. You need to be focused and alert when making decisions within your business. You want to give the best you have to your business so in turn you need to give yourself the best self-love and self-care.

I know this only too well. Whilst getting ready to launch Everyday Lingerie Co, I fell pregnant and was so excited. But as the pregnancy progressed, I started suffering from pregnancy insomnia, which I did not know was a thing.

Every morning between 3am and 4am I would wake up, wide awake and struggle to return to sleep until around 6am. This lasted for the last twelve weeks of my pregnancy. Whilst this was not my choice, it was just part of my journey. As it was when I was making key decisions for the business, it began to really take a toll on me, and I made errors within my work. Errors in some cases that were costly and others that wasted people's time. This then flowed on to me being annoyed at myself and negatively affecting my mindset. I came up with a solution. Bedtime was being moved to an earlier time. I tried to ensure that by 8:30pm every night I was in bed, so I could be asleep earlier and then when the insomnia woke me, I felt more rested. I started putting meditation on whilst lying in bed to allow me to at least relax, even if I was not sleeping.

I was educated on the importance of sleep from my mum throughout my childhood. Then, through working in the bedding and furniture industry for a number of years, I completed countless training programs the respective companies ran, and the findings were the same, so I knew that I needed to ensure my solution was one that would offer my mind and body the rest it needed regardless of the challenge I was currently facing.

In summary, we all have different factors that will contribute to different things on our journey, but rather than seeing a problem and getting frustrated, we need to look at what changes, even small ones, can be made to help the situation. My experience is just an example, this doesn't mean it will happen to everyone, but if you are reducing your sleep to very little and not getting any exercise, the effects will take a toll. Start now by setting great boundaries and practices for your physical self. Just like any athlete, they don't just wake up and decide to run a marathon, do they? They train for multiple hours a day, sometimes for years, to condition their body for one race or meet – you are no different in business.

How do you currently run your days?

Are you getting enough sleep?

Are you prioritising your physical health?

What can you improve on and start implementing to ensure you can perform well every day?

If you are running your startup whilst still working in another job, you need to plan every day and be realistic with what you can achieve. I was doing this initially with both businesses and working full-time and travelling for two to four days every week. My organisation and planning are what benefitted me the most.

I am by nature a very organised person who uses my diary daily, filling it with my to-do lists and appointments. The key is to stick to the tasks set, and some days you won't achieve everything you had set, but that's okay. Move the task to the next day or when you can schedule it in realistically. Life will happen on the journey. Just last week I had scheduled a full day of meetings and tasks but a personal matter arose at around 11am. Everything was put on hold to work through it. I did not get annoyed or angry at myself for not completing my list. The meetings I had booked, I postponed, everyone understood and happily changed the date and time. The following day, I numbered all the actions from most important to least, and at the end of the day, I had caught up on 90% of the day before and completed everything from that day's list as well.

This leads me into the next big area that helped me: my mindset.

Mindset is key to everything you do. If you don't believe in yourself, if you think you can't achieve something, then you will be right. I love the analogy that mindset is like cooking. I believe that if you cook with love, people will taste it in your food. Business is the same for me. If you build your business with love and care, people will feel it in the products or services you are selling and delivering. It is no different to starting and ending your day with a positive outlook. When your mindset is there and positive, you find everything is clearer when you're completing your tasks or actions for the day.

Every day I start with affirmations of some sort. I know this isn't for everyone, but humour me here. Once I open my eyes or start stretching, I start by saying to myself some of the following:

Thank you for the amazing day.

I wonder how many wonderful things are going to happen today.

I am so excited about all the good that is going to happen today.

These are all said before my feet even fit the floor. I then head into the bathroom where I have colourful Post-it Notes laminated and attached to my mirror (yes, I know I did not need to laminate them but wanted to ensure they are legible for a long period of time regardless of the stream in the bathroom). Whilst washing my face and brushing my teeth I read and say another group of them.

I love and approve of myself (thanks, Louise Hay, for this one).

I build my business with grace and ease.

I am passionate about what I do every day.

I am capable of all I want to achieve.

You may think affirmations are not for you, but again, you need to find the right avenue as we are all different. Many people I know have different ways to manage this to get them ready for the day, and you too may need to look for what's right for you.

Could a morning meditation set you up?

Working out to start your day?

Visualisation work?

Stretching?

What are your daily goals?

If you are unsure what will work for you, try different things and see how you feel. If you feel lighter, have a spring in your step or it generally makes you happier, that's when you know when you've found 'the one'.

It doesn't matter what method you use but focus on setting yourself up for success right at the start. Centre yourself to really focus on how it is going to be an amazing day. Every day when my youngest goes off to child care, I say to him, 'See you this afternoon at pick-up, have the most wonderful day.' The other day he was leaving with his dad, and he stopped before heading out to the car and turned to me and said, 'Mum, have the most wonderful day, I am going to, too.' I was blown away. I have been saying this to him for two years and it showed me how I can positively impact him with my words every day, just as I do for myself.

With the added advantage of technology today we have access to podcasts and audiobooks whilst we complete almost any task. I use my time driving to hear the latest audiobook – my genre of choice at the moment is definitely self-love and empowerment. The pep-up I get from authors such as Gabriel Bernstein, Denise Duffield-Thomas, Eckhart Tolle, Tony Robbins, Louise Hay and Rhonda Byrne are so uplifting, keep me feeling energised and offer me different insights to ensure I continue to grow and develop as a partner, friend, mum, business owner and person.

Since I have been writing this book, I have been working on techniques to focus on bringing my positive energy to every writing session I do. I want to ensure that not only do I bring that same enthusiasm I have for my consulting clients, but for every word I write. That I am offering not only some key information, but it comes with the passion and positivity I would have if you were standing in front of me and we were discussing these same principles.

Each night at the dinner table, no matter who is there or if we are out, my family ask each other two questions:

1. What was your favourite part of the day?
2. What are you most grateful for today?

We use this as a reminder to reflect on the day, and everyone, no matter the age, seems to really enjoy it. Sometimes, when running your own biz, you can forget to celebrate your wins, so this is your chance to look back over the day and acknowledge and celebrate it. If you live alone, you can always write these in a journal each day so you can ensure you reflect and celebrate.

Once the day is done, off to bed I go, and again, before I go to sleep, I either write in my journal or I will complete some gratitude work. I do this to ensure I acknowledge myself and my achievements. This is not about someone else offering me acknowledgement, but allowing me to do this for *me*. I can be my own worst critic so instead of focusing on what I did wrong, I end my day with all the things I did right and what I have around me that I am blessed to have. Some days I give thanks for hot water or electricity. These are all things that I know many times I have taken for granted, so I now finish my day with all that I am privileged to have.

As an owner, if something doesn't quite work out or we make a mistake, large or small, many people can easily say nasty words to themselves like *you're an idiot* or *you are so stupid.* This can really impact your mindset and is not beneficial at all for empowering yourself. This can be backed up by a powerful study I once read – this is not verbatim as I don't have access to the study, but an overview.

A class took two jars of water and filled one with notes of negative words and the other was filled with positive words and phrases. Over time the jar filled with all the negative words started to build mould and was very toxic by the end. The other jar, containing the positive words, remained the same pure water that was first poured in. This blew me away; as humans we are made up of around 60% water, so we need to ensure that we are filling these water capsules with positive thoughts, words and energy to help get the best out of it.

To summarise, your mind and body are equally as important as all the planning and research you do to start your business. Setting the structure and tone from day one will allow you to build great practices. Practices that need to include personal time, whether its exercising, affirmation work or just spending time with loved ones. This is key to allow you to remain focused and complete every task with a clear mind. Remember this journey is a marathon not a sprint.

ACTIONS
- Create your plan for daily self-care, think about sleep, exercise and relaxation.
- Think about how you are going to work on promoting a positive mindset for yourself to set yourself up for success every day.
- Decide how you will celebrate yourself and your achievements

every day.

- Think about authors, podcasts or empowerment techniques that you can use as tools on your journey to help refill your energy levels and keep you motivated and empowered.
- Make a commitment to yourself about how you will keep self-talk to positive words only, even if something messes up.

TIP

On days where everything goes amiss and nothing seems to be working or going to plan, do not blame yourself or others. Take a moment and step away. Things will never be 100% perfect, and blaming yourself or starting negative self-talk will not benefit you. Remember you are doing the best you can, and you need to stop, collect your thoughts, take time if you need and then regroup and work through whatever has happened. You got this, and if in doubt, pull up the classic song by Journey called 'Don't Stop Believin'' and play it over and over.

SELF-CHECK-IN TIME

How are you feeling?

I hope you are feeling great now and working through how you will ensure you take care of yourself along with your business.

Take the time to plan your day, week or month and see how this works for you.

As always, if any of this is feeling overwhelming or you're not ready to work on it yet, leave it here and come back when you are ready.

There are a number of great books and podcasts that you can listen to in order to stay in a great mindset, not just whilst you are working on your business, but for day to day. Below is a list of some of my favourites currently.

- Gabrielle Bernstein – *Dear Gabby.*
- Denise Duffield-Thomas – *Chill & Prosper.*
- Maria Forleo – *The Marie Forleo Podcast.*

NOTES

CHAPTER 14

YOUR SCHEDULE

'If you fail to plan, plan to fail.' – Benjamin Franklin

Organisation and structure are required for anyone wanting to go on this journey. People are always saying they need more time in a day. We all have the same twenty-four hours and we need to look at how we can make this work for us. Start by realising that you do not have to complete everything in one day. Spread it out and complete everything you do well, rather than a tick and flick.

What I mean by a tick and flick is that you can achieve lots of your to-do list in a day, but are you doing them well and to the best of your ability? If you had the choice to either complete ten tasks in a day or complete one task but complete it well so you do not have to go back and rework, which one would you choose?

Everyone runs their schedule differently, and I once read about a business owner who only allocates fifteen minutes to each call as a rule. He sets the objective of the call, so it has a structure before booking and if it is not in his diary, his rule is it doesn't exist.

There are extremes you can go to with your structure and planning. Take Mark Wahlberg's day, for example, it's reported that his typical day runs like this:

2:30am	Wake up
2:45am	Prayer time
3:15am	Breakfast
3:40–5:15am	Workout
5:30am	Post-workout meal
6:00am	Shower
7:30am	Golf
8:00am	Snack
9:30am	Cryo chamber recovery
10:30am	Snack
11:00am	Family time, meetings, work calls
1:00pm	Lunch
2:00pm	Meetings, work calls
3:00pm	School pick-up
4:00pm	Workout #2
5:00pm	Shower
5:30pm	Dinner and family time
7:30pm	Bedtime

This is what Mark found worked for him, and you may already be running something similar for yourself, but if you don't have a schedule yet, you need to start thinking about this to give yourself the best foundation to really achieve your goals. Once you set your structure you then need to have the self-discipline to execute it.

By nature, I am a super disciplined person who thrives on structure and organisation. I have always been routine driven and it has served me extremely well. Being time efficient has allowed me to achieve a lot more in smaller periods of time. This comes back to planning and self-discipline. Depending on what age you are, there will be different things happening around you, and if you are choosing to go down this path, sometimes you will need to miss a few parties or gatherings of some sort to get things done. But if you have planned the vast majority of what needs to be actioned or completed, along with everything else you have on, you should be able to fit everything in and still allow for flexibility.

When you are planning the structure that works for you, you need to think about the key things you need to accomplish, and whether you are a founder who is still working their day job whilst starting up or if your new business will be your full-time job.

If you are working another job whilst building your business, the first thing you need to add to your schedule, diary or planner is that commitment.

Set up your schedule, planner or diary daily. First put in your work commitments. If you are working full-time Monday to Friday, put those hours into the calendar for the time i.e. 9am–5pm is work @XYZ Corporation. If you are already solely working on your business, obviously you skip this step and just start from the next.

Next, add in any family commitments you have or invitations for events or functions you want to attend. Remember, balance needs to be in there, this is part of the previous chapter talking about mindset as we all need time to ourselves and with loved ones.

If you need help scheduling your time for physical or mindset work, add these to the calendar. Some people colour coordinate this so they know what a task relates to. For instance, one client I worked with created the following system:

- Yellow was physical activity as it represented happiness.
- Blue was her day job as she felt it was a calm colour like her job.
- Green was tasks for her new business as it represented the colour of money.
- Family time was pink for love, and so on.

There is no right or wrong with this, it's about what works for you.

Next task was due dates for her business, so she knew the deadlines that had to be met by herself or anyone she was working with.

Then we added the open time slots so she had some time to do whatever she felt like. Add a meeting, read a book, go for a walk, watch TV – whatever.

This, paired with her to-do list that was broken into daily tasks, allowed her to have work-life balance and meant she could achieve more in each day as she was not so overwhelmed by thinking she had to accomplish everything in one sitting.

I personally run by my diary every day. I don't schedule sleep or free time as I know my routine from operating this way for around nine years. I still have a physical diary that sits on my desk every day with tasks noted on each page. They can include tasks others need to complete for you on a specific day. At times I work with a wonderful virtual assistant who helps with scheduling content for me on social media and my blogs to be uploaded to my website each week. I have those all noted in on their due dates, so I remember to follow up and check the task has been completed. My diary is about all actions that I am waiting on from others and tasks I need to complete.

If I do not accomplish a task on the set day, I move it across to the next possible day, taking into account deadlines that may be relevant to that task.

I also include certain tasks in there that can be three months away. This ensures that I don't have to rely on my memory as we are all human and can forget. I found getting things out of my brain and writing them down as much as possible has allowed me to not be consumed so much and stopped me from missing small but important deadlines.

If I have forgotten to add something to my to-do list and I am not at the office I simply grab my phone and send myself an email with a reminder in the subject so I can add it to my diary when I am back in the office.

For the reoccurring tasks, I have them loaded into the relevant dates in my diary to-do list. I do this at the start of each year so they are ready for the year ahead or you can choose to put them in your calendar and have them as reoccurring events or actions. Think about what works for you so you get the best out of yourself and your time.

If you are starting to think about what reoccurring tasks you need to have in your calendar, start with some that I work with, they can be weekly, monthly or quarterly tasks:

- Payroll.
- Social media planners – are you completing these weekly, fortnightly, or monthly?

- Website review – checking to see there are no errors on the websites.
- Social media reviews – have all my posts been loaded and scheduled to go live?
- Blogs – do you need to write them or load onto your website?
- My Business Google updates.
- End of month reporting actions:
  - Financial reports, profit & loss and balance sheet.
  - Stocktake of inventory.
  - Website monthly analysis.
  - Review Google Analytics.
  - Accounting reconciliation.
  - Superannuation – due quarterly.
  - BAS – due quarterly.

ACTIONS

- Ensure you have a diary – either online or hard copy.
- Schedule everything you need to into your diary including work commitments, meetings, appointments, family events and even YOU TIME.
- Allow free time in schedule – this can be so you can move tasks or simply have free time for whatever you want to do.
- Create your basic schedule to break up the times, you can choose to have this for weekdays only or create two, one for weekdays and the other for weekends – whichever works best for you.
- Be self-disciplined.

SELF-CHECK-IN TIME

How are you feeling?

Do you already have a plan mapped out for your day to day to help keep you on track?

Do you like structure and planning?

Either way, if you are a super planner who needs everything methodically mapped out or more of an overview style of person – use that as the foundation and build the structure that will keep you motivated and on track to your goals.

The reason I suggest you take the time to check in with yourself every chapter is to make sure you are not feeling overwhelmed or stressing yourself out in your journey.

Building a business and/or brand can be a lot, especially whilst life is happening around you. You may decide that there is too much happening right now and take the time off from the development phase or you are feeling so engaged and motivated that there is no stopping you. Do what feels right for you and within what you are ready and comfortable to do – YOU HAVE GOT THIS.

NOTES

CHAPTER 15

POLICIES, PROCEDURES AND TEMPLATES

'Clearly defined policies and procedures ensure
expectations are clear.' – Danielle Sady

Before launching your brand, you want to ensure back of house is all ready to go, and that includes policies, procedures and templates for all customer emails, company forms (returns, exchanges, refunds) etc.

Many new business owners think, *I am small, I do not need all of this yet, when I grow, I will get it done.* If you leave these until you start growing, you will probably find that you are too poor on time as you will be focused on scaling your business and won't ever get to them or they will be poorly completed.

This planning also ensures when the first return, wholesale connection or enquiry is received you have your plan and it can be implemented seamlessly and without overthinking.

SET YOURSELF UP FOR SUCCESS

Have you thought about what happens if you become an overnight success and your product or service starts increasing rapidly? Think about this now in the startup and planning phase so you have less to worry about as you start scaling and bringing onboard new team members. These don't have to be hundreds of pages in length, but at least have an outline for them so you have a guide to work with as you scale.

WHAT ARE COMPANY POLICIES?

Company policies are a statement of the rules that govern a company's code of conduct and describes how human resources management will deal with issues within the organisation. Think of these as a set of behavioural standards that all employees, including yourself, will comply with when working for or in your business.

In today's landscape, many companies have social media policies so they can include the conduct that is expected from team members in relation to behaviour on social media. This can include the need to have approval in writing for any posts that reference the workplace or mentioning of others within the business.

Some other areas that policies apply to are:
- Equal opportunity/discrimination policy.
- Workplace health and safety policy.
- Travel policy.
- Code of conduct.

- Pandemic policy.
- Employee complaint policy.

With any of these policies, when you want to formalise them into working documents, please ensure you seek legal advice to ensure they are lawful. This ensures both yourself and your employees are protected.

WHAT ARE COMPANY PROCEDURES?

The procedures in a business are different to the policies as they describe the process through which tasks should be completed.

For example, I have created a procedure manual for how every order is packed for Everyday Lingerie Co. This manual contains images of what each step looks like. This ensures that no matter who is packing an order, the result will be identical for each.

When I first started, I went away on a last-minute trip that could not be avoided and needed the orders for both businesses to be packed by a casual team member. They started at the last minute, and I only had one day to train them prior to our departure. It was seamless.

The team member not only had a copy of the manuals for each business with them that had images showing each step, they also had the checklist I'd included so they could crosscheck the steps in an easy-to-read guide that allowed them to be confident whilst working in the role.

Again, if I had not thought of these actionable steps in my planning phase, I would have been chasing my tail at the last minute stressed as I would have had to create a plan for this area of the business.

I created this for every scenario; if a customer buys one, two, three or seven pairs, the manual shows what box the order will be placed into, how to fold the underwear for great presentation for the customer when opening and how to finish off the packaging to give the best experience.

As noted previously these do not need to be encyclopaedia-size books, but easy-to-read step-by-step guides that are simple and effective. Include images where you can, allow the visual reference to remove any misinterpretation that can occur when communicating through written word only.

If you are someone who creates your own product, this is super useful. You can then potentially bring in a contractor or employee, if your budget allows, to assist, as business owners with handmade products usually struggle the most with time allocation. However, if you have this planned in a step-by-step process then you can open up any time and delegate.

Some keys tips to creating a great procedure manual:

- List the steps in the order they occur.
- Keep wording to a minimum.
- Bullet points if possible.
- Clarity – if you are not sure about what you are writing, then how do you expect others to understand?
- Don't assume anything, include all required details.
- Use imagery if possible.
- Ensure they are up-to-date – procedures can change, update them as required.
- Include a checklist. There are other areas of the business that need procedure manuals, not just the order fulfilment. Think about your customer's experience. You are in business because you are selling a product or service and you will have

customer issues to deal with along the way with both retail and wholesale sales.

Many business owners find it can affect their self-worth personally if a customer wants to return or exchange a product or service, and we can sometimes get into our own head when this happens. To minimise the impact, set yourself up by knowing right now before you even start, that yes there will be some customers who do not like your product or service and will want to return, exchange or cancel their order. This is a part of business – you will never be for everyone.

Plan for this now so you do not get stumped when this moment occurs and you can say, 'Right, this is a part of being in business, follow the steps.' This allows you to hopefully remove the emotion from the experience.

As an example, you receive an email or call and a customer wants to exchange their item in line with your returns policy, how do you handle this? Do you need a form to be filled in? Will the customer need to return the goods back before you issue the exchange or refund? This all needs to be clear and consistent. Planning this out from the commencement of your business allows you to act on the request very quickly and seamlessly for the customer and yourself.

For my businesses, the terms and conditions of use are all listed including the returns, exchanges and refund process on my website under the FAQs. These allowed me to then create my procedures for this area quickly and effortlessly.

Step 1 – The business asks for a message to be sent to the main email, that includes the customer's name, order number and issue they want to address and request photos to be included.

Step 2 – I then use a template to ensure all the details required are there to validate whatever the issue is and show the clear plan of actions that both parties need to take to ensure we resolve whatever it is quickly.

Being customer centric is imperative within your business for both a product and service. More and more businesses are online, and not having the physical contact with customers can be harder for the customer experience, so any potential issues need to be handled professionally and efficiently.

This leads to the set-up of templates. This, again, like many of the areas of your business, is to make your life easier and show you are focused on your customer experience.

Did you know it's reported that it costs five to seven times more on average to get a new customer versus retaining a customer that has already purchased from you? This highlights the importance of your customer experience and ensures the transaction is seamless.

I have over twelve different templates set up across my businesses. I started by creating a list of the possible scenarios that could occur, and then considered what I could streamline to assist with my customer communication.

Key areas to think about:

- Customer returns, exchanges and refunds.
- Faulty products – returns.
- Payment emails – for example PayPal or e-cheque payments which take time to clear or direct deposit payments.
- Wholesale client introduction emails.
- Automated out-of-office replies.

Once I had the list created, I then created a Word document

for each one. This allowed me to create the wording and ensure I had included all details correctly in the template and work out if I needed to add any extra forms with these.

Please note on the template if you are adding attachments so the receiver will be aware and you also have this as a reminder.

Once you have all the wording correct, again, if needed, check with your legal representative. Then I always save the Word documents in a folder and label them TEMPLATE and the template name such as ELC RETURNS. Then you need to create any documents that will be included with this communication. If it is being sent to the customer, ensure that it is on brand with your logo and company details. The key is that all templates and any forms are clear in communication, easy to use and will assist the process.

Once these are all created, any that will be emailed to customers I will first create a draft email with attachments if required. This allows anyone working in the business to have quick access to them. This has saved me a lot of time when I have been working with potential wholesale customers.

My draft email is in the folder with the brand's lookbook and wholesale pricing sheet. I copy this across to a new email and attach the files. I then personalise the email to include the client's name and anything extra that was discussed, or I make note that I may have not spoken with the store owner but the name of the team member I spoke with and how they directed me to email the owner, so they are aware of why and how I am reaching out to them.

Before signing off the email I note that I will also be following up and what period that will occur in, so the expectation is set with the potential new customer.

This entire process takes around five minutes, opposed to around twenty minutes when I am completing a call, leaving me an additional hour of work time for every three calls I make – that is a benefit I really appreciate about planning.

To help you set off on the right foot, here are some examples from my draft emails to assist you with getting started:

CUSTOMER RETURNS EMAIL

Hi *[insert customer name]*,

Thanks for emailing *[insert business name]*, we have received your email.

We are sorry that *[insert what the problem is]*.

Please find attached a copy of the *[company name]* return/exchange/faulty garment form. If you can complete this in full and return the completed form along with your garment(s) to the noted return address on the form, one of our friendly team members will review all the details and be in touch to discuss the next steps.

Please ensure that any garments you are wanting to return/exchange follow our company's terms and conditions as noted on our website in full.

All garment(s) MUST adhere to the below list:

- Returned within thirty days of purchase.
- In their original/unworn condition.
- Original tags attached.

We do ask that all customers opt for tracking when returning garment(s) as they remain the responsibility of the customer.

Once your garment(s) arrive back at *[insert business name]* one of our friendly team members will be in contact to advise of the next steps. In the meantime if you have any questions, please do not hesitate to email our team.

Thank you and have a great rest of the day.

Warm regards,

[Insert your business name or signature.]

OUT-OF-OFFICE AUTO REPLY

Hi *[insert customer name]*,

Thanks for emailing *[insert business name],* we have received your email.

Currently all our team members are busy, but we aim to answer all enquiries within one to two business days, so one of our friendly team members will be in touch very shortly.

Thank you and have a great rest of the day.

Warm regards,

[Insert your business name or signature.]

EXAMPLE OF PAYMENT DELAY EMAIL

Hi *[insert customer name]*,

RE: Order *[insert customer order number].*

Unfortunately, due to you placing an order with *[insert business name]* that was paid via PayPal cheque, we have been advised from PayPal that these funds have not cleared yet, and this process takes between two to seven business days.

What this means to you as a customer: as a business we require full payment prior to all items being shipped, once we receive the confirmation from PayPal that these funds have cleared, we will ship your order.

In the meantime, you can view this 'pending payment' in your PayPal account and contact PayPal if there are any issues. Alternatively, once the funds have cleared, we will ship your order and send across an email containing the shipment tracking number.

Please feel free to contact us via email or phone *[insert company phone]* with any questions.

Warm regards,

[Insert your business name or signature.]

This area of your business really comes back to planning. Planning for today and for growth. Scaling a business is what you want to be doing in the months and years ahead so start building your foundation now. If you only ever want to be a small business that is okay, not everyone wants to be the next billionaire, but help yourself by planning, even if it's just with templates to allow your time to be used in the right ways and free you up to be creative, take on new clients or have more free time.

Whatever your objective is, planning and organisation are key in setting yourself up for success and a great customer experience that will keep them coming back and hopefully turn them into a loyal advocate for your business.

The final part of planning that needs to be discussed is about shipping products to consumers. From time to time there can be issues. Delays, lost parcels and even times when the parcel states it's been delivered but they have not received it, or worse still the product is broken or damaged. It can be a very tricky time and your communication is key to keeping a strong relationship with your customer so you can resolve the situation.

DELAYS IN SHIPPING – LOST, STOLEN OR DAMAGED PARCELS

If 2020 onwards has taught us anything, it is that we need to be patient and understand that peaks can happen in every business, especially in transport. Even before the pandemic, many websites had a clause in both the terms and conditions along with the FAQs noting the company's use of a third party delivery service for all orders. The company noted that the third party may experience delays from time to time and that these delays are not the responsibility of the business and they cannot be held responsible for the unforeseen delays.

I incorporated a version of this within our trading terms and flag this with our customers to ensure that we set accurate expectations. Some customers don't read the details, and we understand that, however if the question is raised, we are able to refer them to these areas on the website as part of the sales process to highlight this.

How can you incorporate this for your business?

Delays in today's world are part of society, but as business owners, we still need to have a good idea of a reasonable time frame. If you shipped a product six weeks ago and the customer still does not have their goods and your carrier is not assisting or able to locate the parcel, you will need to plan how you handle this.

Can you reship the product to the customer?

Can you offer them a refund or gift voucher?

Can you offer a partial refund to compensate for the delay?

What other options can your business offer?

Think about how you would feel if you were the customer,

how long would you be prepared to wait? This needs to be factored in for your brand as you want the customer to go, 'Hey there was an issue with this, but that business went above and beyond to get it sorted,' rather than feeling like the business was not interested in helping finish off their customer journey as best they could.

Just like shipping delays, the customer is not responsible if your selected carrier loses or damages the parcel. Once a customer contacts you, acknowledge this communication as soon as you can even with a blanket email.

Hi *[insert customer name]*,

Thanks for letting us know that your order *[inesrt order number]*, has not arrived, we will investigate this and contact the carrier as soon as we can and keep you updated in the coming days.

Any questions in the meantime please feel free to contact us *[insert phone or email]*.

Warm regards,

[Insert your business name or signature.]

The customer then knows you take them seriously and value them.

You then need to follow up:

Step 1 – Check the tracking and see what that shows.

Step 2 – Reach out the carrier and see how they can assist.

Step 3 – How can you resolve this and ensure that the customer receives a great experience with your brand?

Step 4 – Contact the customer with updates and offer

solutions.

Please don't ring the customers telling them the problems or even blaming others, human errors happen sometimes, and as a business you need to sort that out – it is not the customer's responsibility. Talk to them and offer your options one, two and three and let them decide which works best for them. In some cases, if something has been purchased for a special occasion you may need to give a refund even when it is not in your policy because that's all that can fix the situation.

Here are a couple of issues I have personally dealt with:

A customer calls, it's been four weeks and their product has been delayed and it still appeared as if our carrier would not deliver for three more weeks. The customer had called me prior to ordering as they needed the stock for an event. I suggested express delivery service which cost a little extra but that would definitely work with their three-week deadline. Clearly, I was wrong in this case. So, when the customer called about the delay with their parcel, I completed all the above four steps. The customer was happy for me to refund their shipping costs in full to compensate. This worked out well for them as they now needed to buy things for their event from another vendor but still wanted our products.

Example two: A customer purchased over $100 worth of stock, the parcel was showing up as delivered on the carrier system and even had a signature in the delivery docket. The customer called the next day as they received an email saying the parcel was delivered by the carrier. They checked their property and could not find the parcel anywhere. They called the carrier explaining what had happened. The carrier said they have a delivery signature and they classed this as delivered, nothing further to do. The customer called me and explained the story. I again followed the above four steps. After finding out from the carrier that they would not open a case because they had a signature, I informed the customer we would reship the entire order to her to ensure she got what she paid for.

Within ten days of this parcel arriving, a new order came through our online store from this same customer for almost $300. This customer sent an email saying thank you for the amazing customer service and products and expressed how she would be a loyal customer for life as we went above and beyond. We still have never found where that initial parcel went, but it really is just a part of doing business.

When a product is broken or damaged in transit you need to be ready to ship a new one to the customer as quickly as possible. My moto is: always over-wrap (you have not seen how much bubble wrap and sticky tape I can use around one glass vase) as $5 (double the average that is normally used on those parcels) of packaging supplies is much cheaper than having to send an entire new product.

Collectively, my businesses have shipped over seven thousand parcels and I can count on one hand how many issues we have had, and I believe this is due to the following reasons:

- We use a more reliable carrier – the rates are slightly higher, but they have the service and knowledge behind them.
- We use tracking on every parcel that leaves regardless of if it is standard, express or international.
- We pay for the delivery signature option for all parcels.
- We over-wrap and are super protective of the goods we ship.
  These are all things every business can do but they need to

be planned out, you can even add shipping insurance, you just need to ensure it's planned, costed and completed in line with your business guidelines.

ACTIONS

- Plan what company policies are needed for the business.
- Create outlines or manuals you need to get this started.
- Plan out what procedure manuals you need to have written.
- Create the procedure manuals.
- Plan out the list of templates you need.
- Create the templates.
- Create any forms that are needed for customer communication.
- Create your shipping policy and plans together with customer emails for any shipping issues.

SELF-CHECK-IN TIME

How are you feeling?

You have worked through the bulk of the work, and you are closer to your dream because of the effort you have put in, what are you going to do to celebrate this milestone?

Unmotivated? Time to look at what is causing this. Are you overwhelmed by the workload? Do you need assistance and not sure where to ask? What specifically are you unsure about – take the time to write this down to clarify so you know what is causing you to feel this way. When in doubt, take some for yourself and come back when you feel your are ready.

NOTES

CHAPTER 16

SALES PLANNING & STRATEGY: WHAT, WHEN AND HOW

'A sales plan will give you a road map to how you can achieve your desired results.' – Danielle Sady

In the last chapter we discussed procedures and policies you need to plan out for your interactions with customers, but first you need to build your sales budget and plan your strategy for selling. This is the what, how and when. These steps all need to be measurable and you need to hold yourself accountable for the plan.

What are you going to sell?

When are you going to sell it?

How are you going to sell it?

The first step is to create a sales forecast for your business.

The plan creates the groundwork to enable you to start mapping out the actionable steps you need to take to start generating income. You do not have any data yet so these plans are estimates but will allow you to have a goal to work towards.

Your plans need to be measurable and achievable. Putting random numbers in the planning sheet, like setting a $1million goal for the first year of trade means that you need over $83,333 of sales a month. If your product retails for $50 per unit that means you need to sell 166.66 units per month to achieve this. Do you have that much stock in your warehouse? Can you afford to purchase that?

You already know what your cost per unit is by now and may have already ordered your stock, so let us create an example to work through some sales planning.

Example information:

- Order is for one thousand units.
- Cost per unit is $10 landed.
- Total cost for you is $10,000.
- Sale price is $30 per unit.
- Total sell out is $30,000.
- Cost of shipping/packaging to end user is $2.50 per order.
- Total shipping/packaging cost for sell out is $2.50 x 1,000 = $2,500.
- Stock orders take six weeks for production.
- MOQ is one thousand units per order.
- Please note for this example GST is excluded for all numbers and we have not allowed for merchant fees, please use as example only.

SALES OVERVIEW

MONTH	JULY	AUGUST	SEPTEMBER	OCTOBER	TOTAL
Stock on hand	1,000	990	965	915	1,000
Sales by units	10	25	50	100	185
Units available	990	965	915	815	815
Sales by $	10 x $30 = $300	25 x $30 = $750	50 x $30 = $1,500	100 x $30 = $3,000	$5,500
Cost $	10 x $10 = $100 10 x $2.50 = $25.00 $100 + $25 = $125	25 x $10 = $250 25 x $2.50 = $62.50 $250 + $62.50 = $312.50	50 x $10 = $500 50 x $2.50 = $125 $500 + $125 = $625	100 x $10 = $1,000 100 x $2.50 = $250 $1,000 + $250 = $1,250	$2,312.50
Profit $	$300 - $125 = $175	$750 - $312.50 = $437.50	$1,500 - $625 = $875	$3,000 - 1250 = $1,750	$3,229.50

This example shows you that at the rate you're going, you will double sales every month – if that is the case you will sell two hundred units within month four, four hundred units in month five and eight hundred units in month six. This data will allow you to plan for your next stock purchase. As noted, your production time lines are six weeks, and then potentially you need to add shipping. This would then show you need to start thinking about planning your orders with your factory to ensure you do not run out of stock.

You will need to budget for this in your cashflow plans to ensure that you have the money to pay for this.

When starting out, so much of the budget and planning is based on estimates as you do not have the actual data. Every year I start with my cashflow and budget plans. They are all based on estimates, and I update these spreadsheets with actuals once the month has been completed.

If sales are up, you need to adjust your costs, if sales are down you need to change the forecast and potentially remove some expenses to accommodate the actual position of the business.

Having now set up your WHAT forecast plans, they need to align with your WHEN and HOW plans. Once you map out where, we can then break down the forecasted sales into the areas to assist you to drive sales.

There are several places to target and sell to customers, and working out what one is right for your business will come back to your target audience that you mapped out in the initial planning phase.

Where to find your customers:

Retail – direct to consumer:

- Website.
- Social media – paid advertising and social pages.
- Local markets & pop-up events/locations.
- Storefront.

Wholesale:

- Stockists – retail stores.
- Agents.
- Distributors.

Third party sales:

- Online marketing places such as Amazon, eBay and Etsy.

Selling retail direct to the consumer has its pros and cons. Your brand experience will be of the highest level with this avenue. You are in control of every touch point the customer feels and receives. You can grow your database the quickest. Your database is one of your biggest assets so ensuring you have the strategy to grow this is very important. You can then in turn retarget these customers, offer them loyalty discounts to keep driving them back. They are no longer a cold lead, so they have potential to purchase quicker and at a lower cost within your business.

I once attended a business seminar and the guest speaker was from a large international online business. The owner spoke of how, next to their employees, their database was their most important asset. The reason for this is that they knew, even before the customers did, what they wanted to buy. Their customers had purchased X, Y and Z in the past, so when the company was launching a new product, they emailed all the one million customers that fell into that category, and boom, they sold 400,000 units of a new product within the coming weeks.

They could forecast better, make new product decisions clearer and they ensured that their offerings kept getting more targeted to ensure they offered customers what they wanted.

The cons are that you need to manage the customer experience and ensure that nothing is forgotten so everything is perfect for your customer. This can be time-consuming as you're scaling, but I think it is more a pro than a con, because no-one will represent your brand as well as you.

WEBSITE SELLING

Your website is often the area people rely on most. Getting the traffic to your website is not always easy, there are normally hundreds, if not thousands, of businesses selling a similar product or service, so you need to create a website that is:

- Customer-centric – speed, ease of finding answers to questions such as FAQs and about us.

- Easy to navigate.
- Demonstrates to your customers the why behind your product.
- Is informative.
- Has copy that is emotive, informative and on point for SEO.
- Strong imagery.
- Easy to checkout.
- Easy for customers to find you.

With any product or service, it is not about being the cheapest in the market; customers want value and to understand what is in it for them. I know from my personal experience if an online store I'm shopping with doesn't offer PayPal, in many cases I won't shop there, I find it too risky with the high rates of cybercrime. Or if the website takes a long time to load then I also give up and go looking for a more professional website to shop from, even if it costs me a little more.

You want to make the best first impression and aim for a conversion rate of a minimum of 1% as that is the average online.

SOCIAL MEDIA

We have talked about social media previously; however, it is a sales channel that is there to be used. I am aware of companies that have around 80% of sales through their social channels and others are less than 10%. You will learn what your community likes in the months after starting and will notice how this works in turn for sales when it comes to posts.

Paid ads are also part of this, but they are not always the right answer. I have run paid ads on multiple occasions to see how they worked. Whilst the click rates were great and drove traffic, our overall conversion rate was dismal. Customers' responses showed me that I needed to look at the UX and UI experience and how we were targeting. Many agencies would say throw more money at it, however, I have been fortunate enough to chat with a leader in this field and that was a game changer. The numbers do not lie, with a low conversion it did not matter if we increased our budget, the conversion rate would never amount to what was needed to cover the cost.

Think about this carefully prior to starting and ensure that you are not only looking at clicks and visitors, but also bounce and conversion rates as you may find spending your funds elsewhere will offer a greater return on investment.

LOCAL MARKETS AND POP-UP EVENTS

There are literally hundreds of events that offer small businesses opportunities to have a shopfront that gives you the ability to raise brand awareness and get sales.

These also allow you to have a brick-and-mortar store without the huge overheads. Test the market and introduce your brand on a weekend or short-term lease basis.

These events also give customers an avenue to get to meet the face behind the brand which can be great for customers to really see your passion and the love you have for what you do.

WHOLESALING

Wholesaling is another channel that could be right for your brand. You completed your cost and sales numbers in the earlier chapter and will know if this is an option.

If you have the margin to work with wholesalers, it's a good way to help move greater volumes. Margins will decrease due to this, but the increase in turnover allows you to move through your stock holdings at a quicker pace. The options are wholesaling into retailers, using an agent or working with a distributor.

The advantage of wholesaling is the growth in brand awareness it offers. Seeing a brand in retailers can really showcase to consumers that your brand is valuable and reliable. Some consumers will also visit your website and they may purchase online rather than through the retailer – it can really be a win-win.

This path is more time-consuming as you spend the time contacting or visiting potential stockists, working with agents or distributors, and as mentioned the margins are lower and there could be additional fees involved for marketing material, rebates and/or trading terms that might see you waiting thirty days before receiving payment that can affect your cashflow.

These areas all need to be carefully thought out, and I'd recommend you contact a legal representative if you are entering into any contracts to ensure that you are protected and that the terms also suit your business. It's great to get ten thousand units sold into a department store chain, however if they are all on consignment and you will not be paid for sixty days and need to pay 2.5% of rebates, this can add up very quickly since you are paying for the stock up-front – just something to consider.

Your database will also not be grown in this avenue nor in the third party sales. These businesses will not provide you with details of the customers that your products are sold to, this will remain their property.

There are some amazing opportunities within third party sales. eBay has been around for a long time; Etsy, The Iconic and Amazon also fall into this category.

There are many factors that need to be considered with these options, carefully consider each one and do your research.

There are normally subscription fees, holding and shipping costs along with marketing fees and commissions.

Time to research and see which channels are right for your business.

Once you have decided which channels you want to sell through, you can start breaking up the sales budget across those areas to create your budgets in detail.

Budget example:

MONTH	JULY	AUGUST	SEPTEMBER	OCTOBER	TOTAL
Stock on hand	1,000	990	965	915	1,000
Sales by units	10	25	50	100	185
Units available	990	965	915	815	815
Online – website	10	15	30	50	105
Wholesale – retailers	0	10	20	30	60
Third party	0	0	0	20	20

This allows you to plan for the different events you are running or channels you are using. Having this also allows you to see how you track once the event is completed and in the next financial year. You can see if you have a spike in sales this year will that be achievable for the next year or if you need to book additional markets or whatever you need to do to help grow and scale your business.

ACTIONS

- Create your sales forecast spreadsheet.
- Map out the opportunities you will book to target these sales budgets.

- Review cashflow forecasts and actuals to understand the company position.

SELF-CHECK-IN TIME

How are you feeling?

Have you had a chance to see how you are feeling? There is a lot to cover when starting up a new brand or business. If you find that you are getting increasingly stressed or overwhelmed, take some time to yourself. It could be time to stop working on your project and rest up. You don't have to rush to get your business off the ground. There is no right time, it is about you finding your right time in this process.

If you need to step away, maybe make a note in your diary and set up a reminder that says in one week or a month to start working on this special project again.

If you are feeling empowered and energised as you work through all your actionables, keep going use this energy to push on and keep planning and building out your business.

NOTES

CHAPTER 18

WHOLESALE

'It's always better to under-promise and over-deliver
than fall short of expectations.' – Danielle Sady

I felt we needed to dedicate an entire chapter to wholesaling for product-based businesses as there is a lot to cover.

Wholesale is a great income driver and assists with pushing volume in your business. As with every area of your business you need to be set up for success before approaching your wholesalers.

STEP 1 – CREATE YOUR CONTACT LIST

You have already run the numbers and you have the green light to sell into wholesalers, now you need to build a list of customers to contact. The list needs to be easy to use and straightforward so you can be effective and efficient. There is no point if you have a hundred retailers but none of them are focused on your target customers.

How are you going to find wholesale customers?

Research is key here. Look into other businesses who sell similar products, do they have retail stockists listed on their website? If they do, start researching who the stockist is.

- Is it your target market?
- Can you fill a gap for them?
- How does your offer stand out from what they already stock?

If you're sure that you can offer them something different or a product that aligns with their brand and your target customers are similar then add them to your list.

Your customer list can be created in any format, but there are several free CRM systems that are available that can assist you.

For instance, I use HubSpot for both businesses. I signed up for a free account and loaded all the customers into the system. This gives me a central database that contains all their contact details, any information I found when researching them, notes, actions and tasks.

The best part is that it can be set up on your phone or PC so you can access this cloud-based system anywhere and always be up-to-date. When tasks are created, I receive a reminder email so I do not have to remember who I need to contact on any given day. The system also allows you to export all your data and can import large database spreadsheets to help with importing.

I would suggest when setting up the customers, decide on a scale or level system so you know who your priority customers are that you want to target first and second and so forth. This way you break it down into smaller parts, rather than trying to call everyone in one hit and getting overwhelmed. Wholesale takes time, you need to build your relationship, so allow for this.

STEP 2 – CREATE ALL THE ASSETS YOU NEED BEFORE YOU START MAKING CONTACT

When you have your first interactions with a wholesaler you need to be prepared and have all your brand assets ready so they can be shared in that first meeting or sent in an email following.

The brand assets include:

- Lookbook.
- Wholesale price list – any discounts offered.
- Wholesale order form.
- Contract or agreements applicable with all terms listed.
- Samples.

The lookbook is really a way to introduce your potential client to you, your brand and your range. It should have the same look, feel and tone as all your brand assets and offer all customers the opportunity to read and start building an emotional connection to your brand. I would suggest not adding pricing to your lookbook, especially if you are printing them as you don't want it going out of date and then be a waste of money.

They can be created as hard or soft copies; many brands also add them to the website and allow both retail and wholesale customers to review.

Your lookbook should contain:

- About us – stories about both you and the brand.
- Product overview.
- Images of products with full descriptions including colours, sizes, product code, product names.
- Full contact details – phone, address, website, social media handles.

Next create your wholesale pricing sheet; this document can

contain as much or as little information as you want and can double as an order form, or you can keep the two items separate.

Must include:

- Date the form was created, this allows you to ensure that all customers have the up-to-date price list.
- Logo and company name.
- Contact details – they may wish to call you so make it easy for them to get in touch.
- Pricing by product, SKU or product code, unit price (not if pricing is included or excluding local applicable taxes), if there are multiple sizes or colours available list each one.
- Trading terms – MOQs, shipping details (summary of key points).
- Discounts if applicable – order over $500 for free domestic shipping etc.
- How to order – do they email you, fax, call? Be specific.
- Suggested retail pricing can be included if you wish, however, every retailer can decide their own pricing.

Then you need an order form or a plan for how the customers can place orders. I suggest that you have two to three avenues for customers to place orders and you will learn which one suits each customer as you get to know them.

Ordering options:

- Direct through your website – customer has an account and receives wholesale discounts that automatically get applied.
- Order form – they can email, fax or call. The key is making it simple for customers to order from you. They too are running a business and need to maximise their time and be efficient so they can work on their own business.

If you want to create a trading term agreement or contract, you need to start now and contact your legal representative to help you finalise this to ensure that the agreement is legal and protects both parties.

The advantage of creating this agreement is that all the terms and conditions of sale are outlined for both parties before you begin working together. There are no longer any grey areas that can cause issues along the way.

Trading agreement inclusions:

- Details of both parties: trading names, addresses, registered business numbers, contact details.
- Outline of purchasing terms – MOQ, discounts, payment terms.
- How to place orders.
- Refunds, returns or exchanges – if the store has an issue with your product what the process is and how to handle this.
- Marketing – can your imagery be used on their social media or website?
- Signatures and dates agreements are completed.

Finally, you need samples of your products to assist with selling them.

Everyone runs their samples differently. If you cannot visit a store to show the samples to the potential customer, how are you going to share with them a physical product they can touch, feel and/or use to really get to know the product?

Can you afford to send samples out to potential clients?

Will you offer them a discount on their first purchase if they buy a sample?

Will you offer a piece free of charge with free shipping and they can buy additional at wholesale pricing?

This needs to be factored into your plans. As a newer business, you may only have small stock volumes available for sale so shipping samples to fifty potential wholesale clients will see you erode your entire profit margin and cost you shipping on top.

STEP 3 – INITIAL CONTACT

Your first contact with your customer needs to be professional and planned out. Have some notes to ensure you can clearly and easily cover all the information in your first contact.

Many people are happy to start with emails as their first port of call; I personally think it can be a harder way to create relationships so I am more focused on in-store or phone calls for my initial contacts. This way my email is not lost or sitting in spam wasting away while three other businesses have picked up the phone to contact that same store.

- Call first and introduce yourself. I like to take note of who answers the phone so I can address them by name.
- Introduce yourself and state where you are calling from – *[insert business name]*.
- Tell them the reason for your call.
- Ask if they are the owner or manager or if the owner or manager is available to talk to.
- If the relevant person is not available, ask for their name so you can record this and then see if it's best to follow up with a call/email later. Add this into your CRM/database system and record the follow-up task into your diary or task list to ensure you complete the follow-up when stated.
- If they are available, wait to speak with them:

- Give them your presentation.
- Who are you?
- What is your company name?
- Why you are calling.
- Ask questions – get to know their business, you have researched them but they know their business better than anyone and what you saw in store or online might not be the norm. Learn as much as you can so you can see how you can add value.
- If possible, book a time for a product presentation for them to view your product range.

Whether you get to speak with someone or not, it's always great to send a follow-up email to ensure they have your contact details available to them following the call. The email is a short summary of key points covered in the call along with a lookbook or any visuals references for them to review.

Then add all the relevant notes to your wholesale database to make sure that you are always up-to-date.

Several people have noted over the years they find this cold-calling quite tough, and that is true some days. When you hear NO constantly it can be deflating, but you need to keep pushing through because you will get some yeses and that is exhilarating. It's also great practise for stating your elevator pitch, and in the long run the advantages will outweigh the disadvantages. Remember, I said it before and I will say it again, no-one will represent your brand as well as you will, let them see you. It's okay to be nervous, shy or even scared. Everyone has been for some reason or another, but this is like everything else you do in life, the more you do it the easier it gets.

STEP 4 – THE FOLLOW-UP

After you have made your initial introduction to your potential wholesale customer, you need to follow-up. This could be via a store visit, call or email and will all depend on what conversation took place in your previous interaction.

Stick with the format you agreed to and the time frame you supplied, this shows that you are professional and dedicated. If someone waits weeks or months to return my call or follow-up after our last interaction, I think they are not reliable and tend to move into a different direction. This is business and we want to ensure we represent the brand to the highest standard.

Whichever way you have agreed to, ensure you do this within seven days. You don't want too much time passing from your first connection to your second. This next contact will guide you on how to proceed.

If it turns out the customer is not interested right now, ask if you can touch base in six months and see if anything changes. Most of the time they will be happy with that. Add that in your follow-up tasks for six months' time.

If they are interested in proceeding, make a plan with them and include specifics to ensure you are both on the same page.

Action all steps that are agreed to.

Payments are one of the most asked questions I get.

Should I offer trading terms?

What discounts should I offer?

Is consignment worth doing?

There is not one right answer for every business. You have a different plan for every business, however, when you are starting out, COD or full payment prior to shipping is best to ensure your cashflow is there.

The larger the wholesale customer, the greater the trading terms normally are, and this can put a large strain on your cashflow and erode margins quickly, so think about this carefully before presenting to these retailers.

Start small and set yourself up for growth, both with your cashflow and buying power.

The second most asked questions I receive is about shipping stock to wholesale customers. Again, there is no right or wrong. You need to understand your numbers. Go back to your costs, if the customer orders $500 of stock from you, how big is the parcel weight and measurements? What will that cost via your carrier? Can you factor that in?

If the customer is local to you, you could potentially offer pick-up or deliver it yourself.

Plan this out with your numbers.

ACTIONS

- Create your list of potential customers.
- Decide how you will track your database and tasks.
- Create all the brand assets for wholesale.
- Create your basic blurb for the initial contacts.
- When the time is right and stock is available, start contacting potential customers.

SELF-CHECK-IN TIME

How are you feeling?

Are you empowered and ready to keep working through your plans?

Do you need to take some time off from the information overload you are feeling?

If you answered yes, amazing, I say this because you are actually checking in with yourself and listening to how you feel, and that is fantastic.

If you're stuck, take some me time. Visit a day spa, hang with a friend, put away all your work things and spend however long you need away from your work for the time being. When you are ready, come back.

If you are feeling revved up and ready to keep going, read on and keep building.

NOTES

CHAPTER 19

LAUNCHING

*'If you don't have an audience, who are
you launching to?' – Danielle Sady*

Everything you have done up to this point is to build towards
your launch. Sourcing stock, building a website and your sup-
porting documents, running your social media. However, having
an audience and creating hype for your launch is an equally
important step as the rest.

Without building the hype, you are missing out on having
genuine audience interest.

The launch and hype go hand in hand.

Your launch does not have to be an over-the-top affair with a
rented-out venue or a major PR stunt, but it must be something
real and meaningful to your brand.

Your database is key, start building your database for your
brand as early as possible. Whilst your website is being built
in the background, your landing page can have your logo with

a *Coming Soon* message that invites people to sign up for the newsletter. Do not wait to start building your potential client list and don't waste an opportunity. Use this page to tell them what's coming, when and what it will do for them if they sign up.

Offer:

- A pre-launch offer.
- Special discounts.
- Launch details – will you have a competition or giveaway?
- Everything that you will offer for them, why they should not miss this opportunity.

When I launched ELC we actually did a pre-launch competition and there were three winners each receiving a $50 gift voucher for the store. This allowed three new customers to try the range risk free. Two of those winners have purchased more than two times since then, totalling more than $200 in sales so I more than doubled my investment from them, and they have even written reviews for the business across my socials. They trusted my brand because we authentically cared about them and offered them something that would be great for them.

Your social pages are there to help as you get set up.

The opportunities present in social media to help build hype for your brand building to the launch are fantastic, and used right, can really build momentum. If you have the time, you can spend hours commenting on other posts to get more screen time for your account or you can try out different hashtags for your posts to see what works for your brand. The best part is you can use these platforms to show the brand or product building up to the launch e.g. the behind the scenes #BTS.

We posted a lot of behind the scenes from the first weekend photoshoot. We didn't show any products but more of what was happening in hair, make-up and everything else. This saw a growth of over four hundred followers on Instagram alone in twenty-four hours. This meant we had four hundred more people to showcase the launch countdown to and get them on the website. Our first day saw what is considered a good conversion rate and close to four hundred people on the site. Within the first week we had our first month's sale budget sold and already a returning customer with a high conversion rate. This was all thanks to the power of social media and our customer database.

Some key tips leading up to your launch:

- Be authentic to the brand, build something people want to connect with.
- Be focused on how your target market will feel, not what you want.
- How will you be able to use this event to create content to share on social media to keep building the hype?
- Can I collaborate with another person or brand to get more exposure?
- Do not be afraid to go live or put yourself out there so people can connect with you and your reason for the brand.
- Remember to highlight HOW it will make their lives better.
- Potentially pitch your story to the media, press or TV if you have a great hook.

And most importantly, enjoy finally getting to share your product or service with the world. You have worked so hard to get to this point, celebrate all the wins and know that every business owner before you has stood in your shoes, had a moment similar to this before they launched, so take a breather and enjoy – you have got this.

ACTIONS

- Plan your launch time line.
  - List all the pre-launch activities you will be running.
- List of pre-launch plans.
  - Social channels and what content – time for posting.
  - What do you need to ensure you have prepared for the activities (images, stories, videos).

SELF-CHECK-IN TIME

How are you feeling?

Remember that this is a marathon and not a sprint. Take your time and have time off when you need it. If you are feeling like it is all too much, set up YOU time and go do something that is relaxing and helps build you up.

If you are smashing out your planning and loving everything you are doing, keep going, but remember to also enjoy life, don't let it pass you by.

Whichever way you are feeling is correct, there is no right or wrong to any question in this book so listen to how you feel and make sure you regularly check in and reach out for help as you need it.

NOTES

CHAPTER 20

SELLING THROUGH THIRD PARTIES

*'Behold the turtle, he makes progress only when
he sticks his neck out.' – Bruce Levin*

You have launched or are about to launch and need to think about additional places to sell all your stock to.

Selling stock is not just about wholesale customers and your website, it's about the different channels that are available in this technological world we live in, which is an amazing asset for all business owners. These channels are a combination of both B2B and B2C, meaning you may be retailing or wholesaling.

Possible sales channels available:

- Standard wholesale chains – as discussed in our previous chapter.
- Agencies or sales representatives.
- Trade shows.
- Website – online.

- Markets.
- Pop-up events/stores.
- Third party online marketplaces (i.e. Amazon, Etsy, eBay, The Iconic).

AGENCIES AND/OR SALES REPRESENTATIVES

If you are a one-person business this can be a great option for your brand to get the coverage with retailers you need, but there are pros and cons with this method as per the others.

The benefits are that someone will be on the road presenting and selling your product on your behalf, and you may find, as they already have a relationship with key retailers, that you can gain clients quicker than if you were starting from scratch.

The cons in this are you have to remember that sales reps normally have a portfolio of brands that are being presented so you won't always be the priority. Also, it won't be *you* selling your products so some customers won't receive all the knowledge you have on the sales call; and finally, you will likely have to pay commission to the salesperson, so this needs to be factored into the margins when you create your costing.

You also need to have a strong communication with the representatives or agencies so they have all the up-to-date information with them as you offer sales or have pricing changes and new stock lines (or if sell-outs happen).

Relationships are key here to really help your business thrive, and always have contracts in place.

TRADE SHOWS AND EVENTS

Taking part in trade shows is a great way to showcase to the industry that your brand has arrived. Like markets, you will need to pay a fee, and these can range from a couple of hundred dollars to a thousand depending on the size of the event and location. Events that have larger followings and attendees tend to cost more.

Many trade shows are only open to trade or wholesale customers so you will need to assess the customer list to review how these fit with the stores you are wanting to stock to, if at all.

Key things to think about are: what stock you need to bring to showcase your range, cost of the stand and the display, how you will staff the event and how you will take orders.

Plan for how you will sell at this event. It could be a pre-order opportunity meaning you take the order and get deposits for stock that will then be delivered one to eight weeks after, giving you a great opportunity to gain cashflow for the business. As with any event, there is never a guarantee of orders so this needs to be a planned and costed risk for your brand.

LOCAL MARKETS

These are a great tool to connect directly with customers who are in the market without investing in a long-term lease or high overheads. This will be for a day or two normally over a weekend.

Look up markets within your local area via council websites, newspapers, or online via Google or networking groups to see where others within your category have been selling their products or talk to vendors at your local farmers' markets to see how they find events. Networking within this space will help you to find better avenues.

Most of these events will incur small fees for your space to be secured, and what budget you have for these activities will depend on your cashflow so be wise, not every market will be the best event for your brand, always refer to your target market.

With these events you need to be set up with stock on hand and payment options for your customers, so think about all the options to make it easy for customers to shop with you and make your event a success.

POP-UP STORES

Pop-up stores are another name for short-term leases. They can be for a few days, weeks or months. These can be found through local real estate agents or on real estate leasing websites.

This is another opportunity where you can connect directly with your customers and you can potentially sell a great amount of stock in a short period.

When looking at this avenue, remember to cost into the budget for this event the cost of rent, staffing and set-up. Remember to check there is an internet connection so you can put orders through and payments can be taken via your EFT system as well as a cash float.

THIRD PARTY MARKETPLACES

With great marketplaces popping up around the world, there are even more opportunities to push your product and brand and reach millions of customers per day. But you need to understand that just because you want to head down this path doesn't mean it will be financially viable for your business, or the market might not have a place for your brand at present.

eBay is a great marketplace to list on it, and there are great opportunities if you are on certain website hosting platforms such as Shopify to automatically load your catalogue across to this platform. But you will need to spend the time to enter all the data and product descriptions to give yourself the best chance of success.

I personally tried it for a small time and received a few sales, but I wasn't actively working on building this channel so I got very minimal return from it. Others I know have shown me that this is one of their highest-performing sales channels and they manage this through their Shopify store so the fulfilment is seamless for the consumers. They really did their research on the platform before launching, seeing what other offers in their categories where available. They looked at what they needed to offer to stand out from the crowd and used this research when they decided to launch on the platform, and they actively update this platform with the same care they do for their website. This way the customers they are reaching receive their brand's highest standards.

The great thing about eBay as a channel is that you receive all the customer information for your database, so you gain a greater understanding of the consumers you are working with. Remember your data and database is priceless.

The Iconic is another great example for a high-traffic marketplace. Many new business owners, including myself back when we started, thought it was as simple as just getting in contact with the business and telling them I had a product I thought we would be onboarding and that was it, we'd made it.

The Iconic has been set up to think about their customer and really range the brands that offer variety and diversity in the products they advertise, so not every brand that applies will ever make their debut on The Iconic.

When you are making your pitch to The Iconic, do your research. What are they currently offering? How can you offer something different? Talk about what the customer will be getting that will improve their lives – are you unique, where are you made?

Do not be disheartened if they say no the first time. You may need to reapply numerous times before the answer changes, and sometimes it just won't be the channel for you, that's okay too, but if you want to, try to build a strong pitch that shows you understand their business and how your brand will add value for their consumers.

If you do successfully partner with The Iconic you will need to be prepared for the costs associated and the terms of trade. If you are dropshipping, you have certain guidelines and time frames that need to be adhered to. Can you can meet these requirements in your business? And I suggest you have your lawyer look over any contracts that you are thinking of entering to help you understand the expectations and if it is the right choice for your business.

Now, let's talk Amazon. There are many companies and individuals talking about Amazon and the benefits, some even stating they have made millions of dollars with Amazon, which is a fabulous achievement, but you really need to understand what and how this works. I have spent many hours looking into the options and possibilities for my brands with the Amazon platform and love the knowledge I have gained from the exercise, so I wanted to share this with you.

Amazon Australia launched in June 2018, and it has been on a growth steroid since, with the ecommerce leader reportedly breaking through the billion-dollar revenue mark in Australia after sales doubled in 2020 as the pandemic created a surge in online buying. Originally opening as an online bookseller selling the world's largest collection of books, within the first two months of trade the sales were up to $20,000 per week. Currently, it's estimated that amazon.com has over three hundred million active users and ships around 1.6 million packages every single day.

The reason I am telling you this is there is a big difference between Amazon Australia and Amazon US. To access the users, you really need to start by looking at the US market first if that is possible for your business.

Here are some key tips that I have learned in my research from Amazon specialists.

You can represent a brand or a private label. The difference between them is that a brand is like XYZ dog toys, you design and manufacture your product specifically for your clients. A private label is a product you purchase and add your branding to.

The top performing platforms are:

1. Amazon US.
2. Amazon UK.

I was advised, that if I was interested in this path, to focus my attention on the US marketplace as it's the largest shopping group you can appeal to and offers more tools on the platform due to the users and age of the platform.

Like any new platform, once you understand the foundations

you will be able to work with additional platforms, or in this case countries, as they all have their foundations from Amazon US.

There are then two systems for fulfilment. You can either ship the orders yourself, or make use of the FBA (Fulfillment by Amazon) service in which you outsource fulfilment to Amazon.

The FBA service takes a small percentage of your profit to cover the costs of fulfilling the orders. The cost is calculated based on the size and weight of your product and the amount of inventory they will be holding; it is like paying for warehousing space at a 3PL. There is also a monthly fee that needs to be factored in.

With Amazon, like any Google system, there is an algorithm. This platform works similarly to your website and the SEO set-up. The more descriptions and keywords or phrases you include, the better your listing will rank.

Things like barcodes need to be on your products prior to working with them and you need to be prepared to understand that you won't be receiving as much customer data with the FBA system, as they will handle all the customer interaction.

There is a chance that some customers may decide to come across and shop directly with you, but there is never a guarantee.

Overall, all of these systems have pros and cons, and you need to spend time researching and costing out what potentials will work for you. If you are stuck, reach out to experts in these fields to ask them questions or book a mentoring/consulting session so they can help you get started. It is always cheaper to spend the time with experts who can offer correct advice than trying to push through, not knowing the facts, and instead run your numbers for every avenue to make sure your dollars and cents add up to profit in the bank.

ACTIONS
- Research local markets you think may be suitable for your brand or service.
- Research trade or event shows in your category.
- Research eBay, The Iconic and Amazon to see if they will be a suitable fit for your business.
- Search for expert coaches in the areas you are interested in.

SELF-CHECK-IN TIME
How are you feeling?

Take the time to check in with yourself every chapter to make sure you are not feeling overwhelmed.

This chapter can be left until later in your journey, you do not need to complete all of this now but think about this and potentially come back to it later.

Have you celebrated any milestones in your business yet? When was the last one? Take some time to champion one win you have had, personal or professional, in the coming week.

NOTES

CHAPTER 21

YOU (EDUCATION AND GROWTH)

'If you want to stay in your comfort zone, then neither you nor your business can ever grow.' – Danielle Sady

You are the biggest asset to your business, and you can also be the biggest liability. I am a massive believer in how you react to a situation can change everything. For instance, if I wake up and it's raining outside, so many people would say, 'Oh no, it's a miserable day.' I look and often say, 'Wow, what a beautiful day to stay inside and do … *[fill in the blank].'*

This then sets my intentions or vibe for the day. Am I going to be lacklustre in my energy or am I going to *carpe diem* – seize the day? Regardless of the circumstances around me, I always have a choice with how I feel about the day, and this is no different in my businesses. I know that not every day can we all be positive bubbles of unicorns and rainbows – trust me, after suffering postnatal depression I know this all too well – but we do have a choice about the level of energy and enthusiasm we put into our business and ourselves EVERY DAY.

At the beginning of my business journey, I thought I knew everything. Boy, was I wrong. I learned from every role I have had in my career and from my parents, and the greatest amounts of learning have happened by opening our businesses and having shit go wrong.

Each day walking into your business, things can go exactly according to plan or sometimes things will go awry. How you handle them will make all the difference. If you have the right network, knowledge and persistence, this will help you to no end.

You will never know everything that you need to know when you start (and even as you become an owner long-term), none of us do. There are so many conversations I have had with my dad in my adult journey thinking he knew it all, but surprisingly he had to learn a lot the hard way. He taught me through his actions more than anything that I needed to be self-aware enough to know when to further educate myself. I am blessed, like you, to have the world at my fingertips with the World Wide Web and I often use this tool to look up many different areas to better understand a certain topic and to find experts in areas that I lack the knowledge and skill set in.

We are all knowledgeable, but without further growing our skills and knowledge we will remain in the same place and in turn so will our businesses.

I have completed around twelve online courses made up of education courses, certificates and diplomas in the past six years. Some are small and quick, others are longer, but they all have given me a greater understand of a specific area of business and myself. In conjunction with this I actively look for new books, podcasts and networking groups so I can continue to evolve, for myself primarily, but also my family, business and friends.

Self-education, for me, has become something I really love doing because the courses or training I have focused on are areas where I lack understanding and knowledge, which allow me to then complete tasks within my businesses that normally I would put off because I wasn't good at them or did not have enough knowledge to really complete them well. This for me is always hard as I can be a perfectionist, and when I do something half-assed, I get disappointed that I haven't completed the task well enough.

This has also led me to look at mentoring and coaching very differently. I love working with mentors and coaches that offer a different point of view and skill set. Some coaches have been the opposite of me in personality, however, their calm and nurturing nature allowed me to destress within the sessions to really take the time to listen and learn.

Regardless of who I have worked with, the commonality between them all was that they held me accountable in my actions. They never gave me all the answers to my questions, instead, they gave me strategies to work through them myself.

I discovered that in order for me to learn efficiently, there are a couple of key things I need:

- Engagement. I need to form a connection with the book, speaker or program quickly.
- Tone of voice. If it's audio, this is very important; having a drill sergeant will only get under my skin and cause me to shut off.

- Note taking. I may never read them again, but writing notes down seems to allow the information to be absorbed better and I have notes to refer to later in the event I need them.
- The information needs to be provided in a logical order that flows, as I am an analytical person.

Have you ever thought about how you learn best? Take some time and think about this, this will enable you to narrow down the type of mentoring, coaching or self-education you can look for to assist your continual growth for the good of you as a person and especially your business.

When you are looking for coaches, mentors or consultants, use your learning styles when you chat with them for an introduction, as the more the educator understands about you, the better you can see if they are the right fit to work with.

With anyone I coach, I also talk about the accountability that I maintain. We build plans and time lines, and the dates we agree to need to be meet. You need someone who will ensure that you also are held accountable, because if you don't you will have implications in your business and in turn you will probably be wasting your money working with your coach or mentor.

Know that if you head into coaching or consulting, this is not about the person you hired doing the work. It is about someone who is going to act as your 'wing person' and will assist you in working through tasks that you are struggling with, help build your knowledge and most importantly ensure you are accountable for your work.

Outside of your continued education and learning, you need to continue to build your network. This can be in person or online.

Look for events or groups that will offer you great access to people around the world that you can learn and grow from. You may even meet some new friends. With most business networking groups, everyone is focused on connection.

Connection to others, connections with fellow business owners and connections to feel like they are part of something. Often when building your brand it can be lonely as most startups don't have the funding to pay for employees.

With networking groups there are so many great questions asked, and the level of detailed answers you can find in the group is phenomenal. I know personally that I can, on average, learn at least one new business tip a week. It can be as small as how to get a blue tick for your social media account or something that you can do on a Shopify page to do XYZ. It may not be relevant to my business today, but it may help someone I meet along the road or my business in three months from now.

The best part of being in these groups is the positivity and celebrations that are shared. Someone launched their book last week and they became number one on Amazon in their first days of release. The person published this in the group and there were over 150 comments within hours of it being posted, so much support. When the chips are up or down, you can turn to others who may have the knowledge or support you need, and as I mentioned, you may even get a friend or two or a business collaboration out of it.

ACTIONS
- Listen to a podcast that motivates you.
- Plan out your weekly self-care.

- Look for networking groups (physical or online) that you can join.
- Think about areas that you want to be further educated in and potential training, courses or consultants/coaches you want to work with in the future.
- Create a vision board or something similar that will act as a reminder of things you want to do for yourself to grow personally and professionally so you can keep referring to this.

SELF-CHECK-IN TIME

How are you feeling?

Is there a fire in your belly and you are jumping for joy with everything you have going on?

Are you feeling okay, but not sure where to head to next?

Or are you completely out of your comfort zone and starting to feel the anxiety building?

If you answered yes to one or more of the above, that is incredible, as that means you are self-aware, and from here you can work through how to move forward.

Jumping for joy, use that energy to keep building your brand and yourself up with that self-love and spirit.

If you are okay, take the time to reflect on all the chapters and review what you have worked on so far to figure out your next steps.

Stuck and anxious, first things first, stop working on your business and spend some time now on you. Try to complete some relaxation exercises or mindfulness practices. It needs to be about you to help you really relax so you can then have a clearer mind to allow you to decide your next moves.

I spoke to a colleague the other day and they shared that a podcast they listened to had mentioned how we get anxiety and depression when we stand still as our energy is stagnant – I felt like this resonated for me personally. When I'm feeling the butterflies in my stomach, a simple walk makes a massive difference to my being, maybe this is something that can help you too.

NOTES

CONCLUSION

'Beginnings are scary. Endings are usually unexpected,
but it's the middle that counts the most.'
— *Steven Rogers,* Hope Floats: The Screenplay

Sitting down today, I knew that I would be finishing up writing this book, and I walked in with the exact same feelings I did the day I launched my first business. The difference is that I know that it's not just about how it begins or ends, it's about the middle that truly counts. A lot of what I have learned over the past nine years is written in the chapters before this.

This book was never even on my radar until around six to ten months ago, when I found my passion was lacking and I felt lost within my world. I could not figure out what made me happy and what I wanted to do with my life moving forward. It was not just because the world around me changed, but more so because I changed. I am not the same person I was when I started – I have grown, I have stood where you are; the energy, the excitement, the fear, the promise of the unknown and certainty that this is what I am meant to do all simultaneously running through my body and brain in complete unison. This is the most indescribable feeling in the world. I wish sometimes that I knew then what I know now as the journey would have been a lot smoother ride. It's only now that I realise it was never about the smoother ride, it was about finding my passion and pushing myself to grow and learn more every day, increasing my network and doing what I love.

I can tick every one of those boxes today and feel proud. Proud that I never gave up. Proud that I pushed myself in ways I never thought were possible. Proud that even when things went well, I still pushed for more. Proud that every one of the people I met and worked with is someone that I can still call today to chat or ask a question of.

The reason for this book is not about telling you what I got out of this journey, but I wanted to give back. So many exceptional people have helped me on my journey to enable me to launch not one but two brands, and the support was so generous in many cases. Not everyone starting out will have the network or access to individuals that I did, so I wanted to make sure I passed it on.

This is what I learned, and I know that you will take the information in here, digest it and put your spin on it, maybe even one day write your own book with tips and tricks, to continue to give yourself the best head start for your new adventure.

Please remember this is my journey, and as you read and research and network, things will change and evolve, so allow that to happen and grow with that. Just because it's printed doesn't mean it will stay this way forever, just as you won't.

The steps are outlined for you to start, and how you use these steps is now in your hands. You may decide that this is not for you; you may now decide with more certainty than ever that this is your path and you're ready to take on the world, or you may be thinking about how to break this down as you're experiencing information overload.

Whatever you decide to do to from here, remember every single business owner before you once stood in your shoes. Not one of them had certainty that their business would succeed or be there forever. Some may have never even got their first business off the ground. You will never know the true struggles of what someone went through to start their business and you will also never know the names of many successful people as they are not blasted across the media, what matters is that you know this is not a race, this is about your journey. Take that journey at your own pace and the only person to compare yourself to today is to the person you were yesterday.

In conclusion, I designed this book so you can read a single chapter of the topic you are interested in learning about or read the entire book cover to cover and learn lots, not just about business but also about my journey so you can use this knowledge to go off and write your own story: your beginning, middle and conclusion. It's your time, you are ready to decide what's next for you.

Good luck, thank you for spending your time with me and trusting me to offer some advice for your venture, and I can't wait to hear about and follow your startup journeys.

Sending you positive vibes and wishing you every success.

Danielle

xxx

🌐 daniellesady.com 📷 @daniellesady